THE BLESSING EXPOSED

"You can have Heaven on Earth"

T. D. BREWER

www.TDBREWER.com
ISBN 978-1-942260-08-0

Design Layout by Cre8 and Design Bloomington, IL

Printed in the United States of America

TABLE OF CONTENTS

A WORD

As I have been writing this book, the Lord has been speaking to me in great volumes. Two of the most profound statements I have heard so far are "My people subconsciously believe Israel has a different God" and "My people believe Israel and the Jewish people are supposed to be wealthy, but they are not".

I was in shock when I heard this from the Lord. I had to meditate upon this in order to take it all in. There are Christians who believe God is for Israel but not for them?! That is truly corrupt thinking as the same Lord is Lord over both the Jew and non-Jew.

God doesn't have a secret contract with Israel or the Jewish people. God has ONE contract to all people who will call Him Lord. Many Christians bought into a very toxic doctrine that ALL of the Old Testament is the Law.

These Christians believe the Old Testament is no longer relevant for today. This teaching has robbed millions of believers from experiencing the promises of God. Instead of embracing the God who heals, I hear many believers say God gave me this cross (this sickness, disease) to bear for His namesake, or we must suffer just as Jesus suffered as a part of our Christian duty.

As humble as those two statements sound, they are slap in the face to Jesus. Jesus suffered on the cross so we wouldn't have to. Jesus took in His own body all manner of sickness, disease, sorrow, sin, poverty and grief. Jesus confirmed this work with His body by saying, "It Is Finished". Jesus didn't lie, but many Christians act like Jesus still has a work to do.

1

No, Jesus did it ALL, and now He is seated at the right hand of the Father waiting for the Church to correct its thinking.

We must come to ourselves as the prodigal son did. He said to himself, "Why am I choosing to live a lifestyle that is less than that of my father's house?" As a born-again believer, we are the sons and daughters of our Father God. We too can choose to live His lifestyle within our world today. The economies of this world are subject to the Kingdom of God. We do not have to wait to experience all that He has until we reach Heaven.

We must press into the Spirit of God to seek the wisdom and understanding needed to succeed in life in this hour. God wants His children to know Him as El Shaddai and God Almighty. It is our revelation of God that is going to equip us to win the World; not some half-baked doctrine that gets our eyes off of Jesus.

As you read this book, it is my sincere prayer that you will experience intimacy with God and walk in His purpose for your life.

Yours truly,

T. D. Brewer

TRANSFIRMATION ™

The **TRANSFIRMATION** ™ **Mentor** is designed to guide you through the process of renewing your mind to embrace the goodness of God. The mind is the door that gives access and permission for our dominant thoughts to become a living reality. The purpose of the TRANSFIRMATION Mentor series is to mentor you in the reality which God desires for you.

> *The LORD is good to everyone and has compassion for everything that he has made.*
> PSALM 145:9 GW

> *For you are God, O Sovereign LORD. Your words are truth, and you have promised these good things to your servant.*
> 2 SAMUEL 7:28 NLT

As you are reading and meditating upon the treasure of revelation revealed within these pages, may your expectation of the goodness of God and the Blessing increase. God desires your life to be a reflection of His Word fulfilled and the promises manifested. The TRANSFIRMATION Mentor will guide you through the Word of God and will reveal to you the life which God originally planned for you.

As we experience life, we allow many things to determine the way we think, speak, expect, and respond. However, not every thought is to our benefit, and neither is every word that we speak. Jesus is the greatest example of one who understood the power of thoughts and words. Jesus is our example of how to live a disciplined lifestyle that produces the results that God desires in our lives.

3

We live in a society where the Word of God has been minimized. As a result, the authority and power given to mankind has been minimized. When an individual does not know who he or she is in Christ and what he or she has received through Christ, that individual will settle for the status quo.

As we study the Word of God, it is quite clear that the lifestyles of the believer and the unbeliever should not be the same. The believer should create his or her world through the power of the spoken word pronouncing the Blessing upon his/her life and praying the will of God.

The unbeliever should be the example of one who will accept whatever life throws his or her way. However, as I listen to conversations and read various writings, I find that believers are saying the same things as unbelievers. As you study and become an ac-tive participant in the content presented in this TRANSFIRMATION Mentor, you will learn to experience the reality of the Blessing and the power of the One New Man.

Stop being conformed to this age, but you must from the inside continually be changed into another form, by the renovation of your mind, to prove what is the good and pleasing and perfect will of God for you.
ROMANS 12:2 PNT

Don't copy the behavior and customs of this world, but let God transform you into a new person by changing the way you think. Then you will know what God wants you to do and you will know how good and pleasing and perfect his will really is.
ROMANS 12:2 NLT

According to scripture, a believer's thinking should not be of the world mindset. Instead, we should think from our position as children of Almighty God. As believers, we are to function from a higher level of perception, understanding, and wisdom because we have the mind of Christ.

For who hath known the mind of the Lord that he may instruct him? But we have the mind of Christ.
1 CORINTHIANS 2:16

Let this mind be in you, which was also in Christ Jesus.
PHILIPPIANS 2:5

The mind of Christ was the mind of the Father. As we operate in the mind of Christ, we operate through the mind of God. We were created in the image and likeness of God to think and speak like Him on earth. For mankind to fulfill the assignment of God on earth, we must be receptive of divine thoughts from God.

"Come on now, let's discuss this!" says the Lord, "If you are willing and obedient, you will eat the best from the land (experience the best life has to offer)."
ISAIAH 1:18-19 GW

"My thoughts are not your thoughts, and my ways are not your ways," declares the LORD. "Just as the heavens are higher than the earth, so my ways are higher than   your ways and my thoughts are higher than your thoughts."
ISAIAH 55:8-9 GW

And now, dear brothers and sisters, one final thing. Fix your thoughts on what is true, and honorable, and right,

and pure, and lovely, and admirable. Think about things
that are excellent and worthy of praise.
PHILIPPIANS 4:8 NLT

The thoughts we meditate on are the thoughts we will give life to. As we meditate on certain thoughts, we are actually watering those thoughts to become a living reality. The mind is like the uterus of a woman. It is a place of development, maturity, and life. The mind is also like soil. Whatever you plant in it will grow. My favorite illustration is that the mind is like a refrigerator. Whatever you place in it is what you will have access to.

As we examine our lives, we must be totally honest with ourselves when it comes to deciding if what we have in our lives is pleasing and acceptable to God, our Creator.

This set of instructions is not to cease being a part of your
conversations. Meditate on it day and night so that you
may be careful to carry out everything that's written in it,
for then you'll prosper and succeed.
JOSHUA 1:8 ISV

What one is generally exposed to is what one will typically meditate on. It is extremely important that we feed and expose ourselves to that which contributes to the plan of God being fulfilled in our lives.

What we meditate on, speak, and demonstrate is a result of our individual choices and decisions. God is not going to force us to think, speak, or do as He desires. We have to make that choice just as the prodigal son did. We need to realize when we are not living in the Father's will for our lives, or we will continue to allow ourselves to live in a pit.

When he came to his senses, he said, 'How many of my father's hired hands have more than enough food, and here I am dying of hunger!'
LUKE 15:17 HCSB

In this story a young man took his inheritance and lived a lifestyle that was to his demise. He envisioned a lifestyle that was fun, exciting, and glamorous. Instead, he lost everything, even his pride and dignity. As many of us do when we are young, he did not accept wise counsel from elders, parents, or loved ones, as he perceived them not to understand.

The prodigal son was one who believed he knew better than his father. Today many of us think we know better than our Father God. As a result we fall into the pitfalls of life that strip of us vision, strength, energy, and hope.

It is vital to our success in life that we receive instruction, direction, and correction from our Creator. The prodigal son chose to go back to his father's house. That was the best decision he could have ever made. In his father's house were love, compassion, provision, safety, purpose, dignity, self-worth, and a sense of pride.

Sometimes when we lack living examples of believers in our life who are prospering under the will of God, we think that it is im possible to live out the will of God. Today God is calling you to become that example for your generation.

Jesus is our greatest example of someone who did not accept

desires less than the perfect will of God. In the Garden of Gethsemane, Jesus was in a place of great decision. At this pivotal moment in time, He said, "Not my will be done, but Your will be done." Jesus's continuous desire was that the will of the Father be done. As we study the Sermon on the Mount, we see that Jesus taught the disciples to pray that the Kingdom of God be manifested on earth as it is in Heaven. Jesus demonstrated to mankind that even though we are on earth, we don't have to live life from this dimension. Jesus showed us that we could be here and still achieve our God- ordained purpose with God's help.

"Our Father who is in Heaven, Your name must at once be made holy; Your Kingdom must now come; Your will must be done right now as in Heaven also on Earth; You must now give us today the things necessary for our existence..."
MATTHEW 6:10-11 PNT

As you are an active participant in the **TRANSFIRMATION** ™ **Mentor**, you will be exposed to the thoughts of God and His original plans for your life.

"Come on now, let's discuss this!" says the Lord, "If you are willing and obedient, you will eat the best from the land (experience the best life has to offer)."
ISAIAH 1:18- 19 GW

A daily scripture, affirmation, and confirmation are conveniently located in the rear of this book to expand your awareness of the thoughts of God toward you. An affirmation is a spoken declaration of scripture that gives it access and life to become a reality in our lives. As you affirm the scripture daily, expect a breakthough

8

in your consciousness of God. The confirmation is an acknowl-edgement of who you are as a result of the Word of God.

The confirmation creates an awareness of your potential and power through the presence of God within. As you speak aloud the confirmation, you send forth the power to create its reality.

For additional understanding of affirmations and the power of speaking the Blessing please read another of my books called Activating the Blessing of Abraham, a power-packed mini book with a vocabulary designed to create Heaven on earth.

INTRODUCTION

As I was in the process of writing this book, I received a phone call from a veteran pastor. He called to explain to me how he had just realized that he had not been taught the Blessing of Abraham and therefore, had not taught it to the people. The morning he called it was like a light just came on for him. He realized how much he had not been taught about the Blessing of Abraham. He had scanned the Bible in his mind from beginning to end and asked me several important questions that morning that he had not thought of before.

This pastor like many others had been taught a Gospel without the Blessing. The Blessing is the missing ingredient from the Church today. I personally believe that the Blessing, missing from the lives of many Christians, is a result of a misinterpretation of scriptures from Apostle Paul's teachings to non-Jewish congregations. Paul was teaching people who were outside the commonwealth of Israel, who had no access to the God of Abraham, Isaac, and Jacob.

Remember that you were at that time separated from Christ, alienated from the commonwealth of Israel and strangers to the covenants of promise, having no hope and without God in the world.
EPHESIANS 2:12 ESV

As a result, organized religion has taught the ways of God as "that's just Jewish culture" or "we don't do that because we are not under the law" or "those are the Jewish feasts and holidays". Those statements have isolated and/or hindered people from experiencing the goodness of God through the Blessing.

This is what I mean: the law, which came 430 years after-
ward, does not annul a covenant previously ratified
by God, so as to make the promise void.
GALATIANS 3:17 ESV

The ways of God have become ingrained in the culture and the ways of Jewish people through the teachings of Moses. Moses reintroduced and taught that which was lost through slavery in Egypt once the children of Israel were set free.

And they will listen to your voice, and you and the elders of
Israel shall go to the king of Egypt and say to him, "The
LORD, the God of the Hebrews, has met with us; and now,
please let us go a three days' journey into the wilderness,
that we may sacrifice to the LORD our God."
EXODUS 3:18 ESV

The first thing God instructed Moses to do was to tell Pharaoh to let my people go, so that they may travel a three-day journey to go and worship the Lord. God desired the children of Israel to know him as the God of Abraham, Isaac, and Jacob.

The teachings of Abraham to the Hebrew people were lost as result of 400 years of captivity in Egypt. Prior to Hebrew children being enslaved, Abraham taught them to worship the Living God and instructed them in the ways of God.

That which we commonly refer to as the Law of Moses was instituted by God as an incentive for the children of Israel to adopt the ways of God into their society and everyday lives. The Law itself was great and the people saw the benefits and rewards from obeying God.

It was the penalty of the law, which we have termed as harsh, that Jesus came and fulfilled. Jesus bore the penalty of the Law, which is commonly referred to as the curse of the law.

Today, we are free from the penalty of the law through the finished work of Christ. But, as a result of Greek influence and the Church of Rome, many believers are still ignorant of the power of the Blessing. Consequently, there are many sick, afflicted, and impoverished believers of Jesus. This should not be so because the Blessing empowers, equips, delivers, and makes rich.

Over the years in Christianity, sickness, disease, and poverty have been displayed like trophies and badges of honor. People bought into the lie that if you are going to serve God you need to suffer and be poor. Many people have been robbed of their God-given purpose and assignment as the pressures of everyday life was greater   than their image of God.

I have counseled many God-fearing individuals in various walks of life who felt like giving up. They had done everything the preacher or evangelist had told them, and yet their circumstances never really seemed to improve. Revelation knowledge of the Blessing changed their circumstances and their lives.

As you read this book, I pray that you will be empowered with revelation to experience the love of God, the grace of God, the goodness of God, and the fulfillment of the promises through the Blessing. We are the seed of Abraham and are therefore recipients of the promises God made to Abraham and his descendants.

And if you are Christ's, then you are Abraham's offspring,
heirs according to promise.
GALATIANS 3:29 ESV

FREEDOM

Several years ago I came to a crossroads in my life. I found my-self at the intersection of average. I was barely getting along, by worldly standards, and then there were the promises of God that I was reading and meditating upon in the Word. Which way do I choose? Do I give it all I had or do I give it up? This intersection may be a common meeting place for millions who struggle with wanting more out of life or who want the best life has to offer.

As a young adult I had big dreams and plans that I wanted to live out. I was excited about life and saw that my future could be what-ever I wanted it to be. That is, until I started sharing my dreams with dream- killers. Dream killers are individuals who have given up on their dreams. They have become somewhat bitter and dis-appointed in their own dead dreams, and so they can't and won't celebrate the reality of your dreams.

I learned that if I was going to live the ultimate life I could not allow others to define my life. I have freedom to become and achieve whatever I can believe for my life. I dream big and encourage others to dream big. I have been criticized and called the devil and/or a false prophet. I don't care what people say about me, because I don't believe their words about me. I believe my words about me!

Each day I speak words of encouragement and empowerment to myself. I stand in the mirror and speak to myself, declaring and decreeing support for my dreams, my goals, and my belief in who I am in Christ. I know what it is like when many people do not be-lieve in you or encourage you. I know what is like when those you have been friends with for years attack you with negative suggestions out of jealousy. I know what is like to think that nothing good can come out of your life.

I remember in my first year of being a senior pastor there were days when I didn't want to go to church. There were several times when I would go to Sunday service and get the hell beat out of me. From the time I walked in the door to the time I walked out, it was one complaint and criticism after another. That got old very quickly. My perception of the Church was different from many others as I knew what it was like to know the love and heart of God.

Today I have an amazing relationship with God. His loves surrounds me and continually overtakes me. There is nothing that comes close to God's love for you and me. No matter how people treat you or receive you, know that God loves every inch of you. God is for you and with you. His plans for your life are great and wonderful.

After I forgave all the people whom I thought would embrace me with the love of God as the new young pastor, God began taking me on a journey of love. I have had the ultimate experience of being able to be light and encouragement to several individuals who wanted to commit suicide or to harm someone else. As I go through my normal day I will encounter random people whom the voice of God has led me to encourage and help.

One night the power was out in my neighborhood and it was just too dark to stay home alone. I decided go to Denny's restaurant to read, however, I was divinely guided to stop at a local gas station to get some money out of the ATM first. When I walked into the gas station, a young man came up to me immediately, saying he liked my t-shirt. He then began sharing events that had happened just moments earlier that night. He and his friend were in town and this friend wanted to commit suicide. When he told him that suicide was not the answer, this friend turned on him and wanted to kill him. I had the opportunity to love on those guys and minister to them for a couple of hours. We shared tears of joy and victory at a gas station because of God's love that came into that situation like a flood. When we parted ways there was evidence that God had been present.

Situations at times can be so overwhelming that we can't see a positive way out. I want to let you know that with God there is always a light at the end of the tunnel. There is hope for a better tomorrow and you can make it in life no matter what. We have the power within each of us to triumph and experience the best life has to offer.

Life is one of those mysteries mankind has been trying to solve for ages. When we were born there was no how–to-live instruction manual given to us. Therefore each of us must be the architect and engineer of our life. We have to take charge and say I am going to live and live well, no matter what other people think.

A few years ago I was at a local high school and encountered an older gentleman who was struggling with everyday life. He was allowing what didn't happen in his past to determine what will happen or not happen in his future. He had a beautiful family and earned a decent salary, yet struggled to see the good which surrounded him. Sometimes we can allow ourselves to become so consumed with the past that we rob our future. Are you robbing your future by continually having an affair with your past?

I could go on and on about the love encounters I had where God was able to remind individuals how much he loved them. Today I enjoy going to church to be that example of love, faithfulness, dedication, and possibility. I use the term possibility as I always desire to be a vision to someone that if they will not quit, anything is possible. I strive to be that vision or visionary that someone can be inspired to live by and follow their dreams.

As I write this chapter in a hotel in Washington, D.C., a couple of blocks from the White House, I am living my dreams. The dreams that were once impossible for me are now becoming a reality. Today I have access and partnerships that I could only image. I have my first patent 100% approved by the United States Patent and Trademark Office. I have formed a company around that patent to bring it to market. As a self-financed start-up, my company has a Chief Financial Officer, our first equity partner, an amazing Certified Public Accountant, and access to some of the largest organizations in the world for guidance and growth.

If you will only dare to dream and act on it in faith, you will see God's hand with your hand. In fall 2014, I set out to publish three manuscripts I had written. Anyone who has self-published knows it is not cheap. So I took a leap of faith to publish five books in total. Three of the five books are in English and two are in Spanish. My out-of-pocket expenses were nearly $11,000.00. I printed 5,000 copies my first printing. I started in faith believing the money would somehow become available to me. I was in the office praying one day when I heard the voice of the Lord say go and check the PO Box.

I obeyed and to my amazement there was a letter from my former employer stating that I could begin drawing my pension. I was shocked and confused as I am nowhere near retirement age. At age 37, I was able to receive my pension eighteen years ahead of schedule to pay for my project. When I contacted them, I was assured this was not an error and that I had to make a choice to draw my pension monthly, wait until 55, or receive a lump sum now.

As a result many people across America have read those books and experienced real transformation. Writing books for me is a dream come true. My freshmen English instructor in college would always tell me I was a horrible writer. When no one else believes in you, choose to believe in yourself and the presence of God within you.

Today I enjoy living on the 18th hole of an Arnold Palmer golf course in a five bedroom, four and a half bath home because of the Blessing of God. When I made the offer on my home people thought I was crazy. I was given a thousand reasons why I couldn't have this house. However, all I needed was one yes from God to be a living witness that God's Word works if your work it.

We have a God who is for us and not against us. We have a God who is holding our right hand saying I am here, I will help you, and I will strengthen you. There is no pain, experience, or disappointment strong enough to rob you of the goodness of God. As I had to choose to forgive others and let love have its place in my heart and life, so must you.

There is a refreshing freedom that is activated in our lives when we forgive others and ourselves. Today I know what it means to have life and enjoy it. Living your dreams, going after your goals, and pursing your passion are all a part of enjoying the journey of life.

RELATIONSHIP 1.0

In order to experience the fullness of the Blessing and the promises of God, one must have a relationship with God. Today we live in a society where people want the goodness of God and the fulfillment of the promises without a relationship with the One who made the promises.

It is clear in scripture that apart from God we can do no good thing, but we were created to partner with God. As we study to experience the reality of the promises in scripture we   realize that those who walked with God walked in the Blessings of God.

The most important opportunity we have in this life is to cultivate our relationship with God. As I write this book my primary focus daily is still to draw closer to God than the day before. I am so thankful for the pastor in Oak Forest, Illinois, who instructed me in a prayer to accept Jesus as Lord of my life. At that moment it seemed as nothing had changed in my life. However, there was a change brewing within that would change my life forever.

For years as a young adult I would ask questions. Is God really real or is this whole Jesus thing one big scheme? I saw many well-meaning individuals going to church, quoting scriptures, and carrying bibles, without much change in their lives. For some, the only change I saw was in their hand or in their attire. There was very little transformation in their heart and/or circumstances.

I would always hear "God is good", but my life experiences had put a big question mark behind that phrase. Each of us has to come to a place where we say to God, "Look, if you are really real, show me. If not, let me know so I don't waste my time believing in the longest running fairy tale in history."

My questions of God were "Where are you?" and "Why aren't you actively involved in my life?" They led   to responses and experiences which changed my life forever. Today I am a very happy man as I have my own personal relationship with God Almighty. I am not living life through someone else's understanding or relationship with God. I can say I KNOW Him as Father and Friend.

For many years I was afraid of God because I thought He was mean and angry. I was under the impression that God was wrath and not love. Today I know God as love through an ever-evolving personal relationship with Him.

I have had some amazing experiences in life that have been both good and bad. However, there is nothing that comes remotely close to the intimate experiences I have with Father God. The love that He has for each of us is beyond expression in words. I honestly have no greater desire in life than fellowship with Father God.

We live in a society that is microwave, fast paced, and self-serving. Our church services have little to do with God and all the more to do with what people think, feel, and desire. As a result we run worship or so called worship services 20, 30, or 45 minutes. Worship has become an obligation versus a response to the love of God.

As a result many are delusional in what they believe concerning their faith and relationship with God. At our church the focus is on what God desires versus what the people desire. If you give people God, they will desire God. If you give the people programs and tasks, they will desire them.

Because of a lack of understanding concerning the importance of an individual relationship with God, many people think their service to God is good enough. God doesn't want our service. Jesus died for us to know Father God, not to work for Him. God wants our hearts.

It is the heart of a person that God seeks and pursues. It is up to each of us individually to make that decision to accept the desire of God and become His child. We only become His child through accepting Jesus as Lord.

The greatest decision I ever made was to say "Lord Jesus come into my heart. Reign over and in my life. I believe you are God's beloved son and you died for me. Today I accept your will for my life. I now live for you and not me."

Sometimes we have to get desperate and sincere to truly receive Jesus as Lord. I know there was a time I prayed a similar prayer looking for an outward experience and then felt discouraged be-cause I could not see anything different with my eyes.

I know I am not the only one who felt that way. I learned to look within as God always begins with an inward work to create out-ward change. I encourage you to look for change within and you will see that God is at work in your life.

Choose to seek and pursue God daily. I came to that place where I said I want what God wants for my life. One of the things God wants for each of us is for nothing to separate us from His loving kindness.

If you want to experience love without limits or conditions, seek God. If you want to experience true peace and joy, seek God. If you want to live a happy, healthy,   and prosper life, seek God. If you want to experience forgiveness and compassion, seek God.

I can't express or impress upon you enough to pursue God with every fiber of your being. God wants to fellowship with you and have an intimate relationship with you. God loves you so much. It is as if no one else exists.

God's love for us is beyond comprehension. As we draw near to God, He will reveal His love for us, and the good things He has planned for us who love Him. As we seek to know Him, God reveals to us that we are His greatest creation, created with a mighty purpose.

Each of us was born with a specific purpose in the mind of God. As we spend time with Him, He reveals that purpose to us and releases us into our individual destiny.

REVELATION 2.0

You may wonder why the title of this chapter is Revelation 2.0. Well, its title is derived from an experience Peter had with Jesus. Jesus asked his disciples, "Who do people say that I am?"

After several responses, Jesus, looking at the disciples, asked them, "Who do you say that I am?" Peter responded with an answer that was quite different from those previously mentioned. Peter said, "You are the Christ, Son of the living God."

Immediately, Jesus responded to Peter, as his answer was not of human reasoning or understanding. Jesus's response was, "Flesh and blood did not reveal this to you." Jesus was almost in awe of Peter's response as he says, "My Father who is in Heaven has revealed this to you."

Jesus explains to the disciples that those who know this revelation and walk in it will not be defeated in this life. Jesus promises today that if we walk in the revelation that He is the Christ (Messiah), we would have victory over the devil, fear, negative thoughts, and the kingdom of darkness.

Jesus boldly proclaims that the gates of Hell will not prevail. This statement "the gates of Hell" is an unusual choice of words for Jesus as you study His ministry. Why did he say such a thing? Jesus was emphasizing the reality of His promise. No matter what Hell unleashes against a person, IT WILL NOT WIN.

Revelation is the key to breakthrough, deliverance, healing, prosperity, and peace. Over the years many people have said to me that you act like you're the only person God has time for, or

God can't bless anyone else because He's too busy blessing you. At that time in my life, I can honestly say I didn't realize it was the revelation that I operated in that set me apart from others who didn't have the understanding I had. I was protected from a lot of denominational teachings which cause many believers to have hang-ups in life that rob them of the will of God.

The Bible says that we go from faith to faith and glory to glory. As believers, we should be continually growing in spiritual under-standing so that we would work the works of Christ and experi-ence the fulfillment of the promises of God.

If a person lacks revelation, he or she will not move in faith or go from faith to faith. Instead he or she will always put whatever it is back on God and not take ownership for the present circum-stances in his or her life.

Jesus taught the disciples to take ownership of their lives and not to allow the world to dictate their life experience. If one is comfort-able in his or her circumstance, he or she will not choose to ma-ture or seek understanding from God. We must seek to upgrade our understanding as we do our cell phones and computers.

The latest technology or cell phone is always on the cutting edge with better and more features than the last. As new cell phones rollout, people will sleep in parking lots and sidewalks for days to get the newest phone on the market. Yet, after spending days or hours waiting for a device that will soon be obsolete, many be-lievers never spend at least an hour seeking revelation, wisdom, and an understanding upgrade from the presence of God. The revelation which God has for us who believe is far greater and much more advanced than the newest cell phone.

God is constantly revealing Himself and making who He is known to all of creation. God, in His loving kindness, revealed to Peter the true nature and identity of Jesus. Then Jesus encourages Peter and the other disciples to never forget that He is the Christ, the Son of the Living God.

In addition, Jesus was emphasizing the power of the revelation itself versus the potential fury Hell could release against one's life. All the fury of Hell is weak in comparison to one's revelation that Jesus is the Christ, the Son of the Living God. You may be thinking, "That is a strong claim". Well, it is a truth that will give anyone perpetual victory when it is REVELATION to them.

What is your revelation of Jesus and does it give you victory? The moment in time when Jesus proposed his question and Peter responded, all of the disciples' revelation was upgraded to that which comes from God. Who or what has framed your understanding of Jesus?

The revelation that Peter revealed publicly is still applicable for us today. Are you due for a revelation upgrade? Well, the good news is that there are no long lines, no shipping delays, or software glitches with God. Choose to ask now and be prepared as God reveals the revelation of the Christ to you.

Honor

For God said, "Honor your father and mother" and "Anyone who curses their father or mother is to be put to death.
Mathew 15:4 NIV

Honor your father and your mother, as the LORD your God has commanded you, so that you may live long and that it may go well with you in the land the LORD your God is giving you.
Deuteronomy 5:16 NIV

Children, obey your parents as you would the Lord, because this is right. Honor your father and mother, which is the first commandment with a promise, so that it may go well with you and that you may have a long life in the land. Fathers, don't stir up anger in your children, but bring them up in the training and instruction of the Lord.
Ephesians 6:1-4 HCSB

What is up with all the scriptures on honor and obedience? In the beginning, God was the original parent to Adam and Eve. It was God's desire that he would have a family that He could fellowship with and love. After God created them male and female, He acknowledged them as good. God was pleased with His masterpiece: mankind.

For we are God's masterpiece. He has created us anew in Christ Jesus, so we can do the good things he planned for us long ago.
Ephesians 2:10 NLT

God the Father created a son and daughter for His glory, pleasure, and delight. He created them with purpose and desired for them the best earth had to offer, which was the same as the Heavens at that time.

God placed His beloved son and daughter in the garden called Eden. In Eden was everything a person could ever dream or desire. God told Adam and Eve they could eat of any tree except one; the tree which contained the knowledge of good and evil.

They had it made. Life was great and God fellowshipped with them daily. As a loving and caring father, God just wanted to be close to Adam and Eve. Then the ultimate day of disobedience came when Adam and his wife ate the fruit from the tree which God had deemed off- limits.

After they ate, the Bible says their eyes were opened. This is very interesting as their eyes were closed at the same time. You may say, "Can your eyes be open and closed at the same time?" Well yes, in this situation. Their eyes were open to a reality which was not the will of God, but their eyes were also closed to the will of God and the goodness of God. They could no longer see through the same set of eyes God saw through.

Once their eyes were open to the counterfeit reality, they hid themselves as they perceived they were naked and exposed. Prior to the vision change, they could see each other only in the glory and through the glory. They only saw each other as God saw them. Once Satan became their stepfather their identity and relationship with God changed.

Now they couldn't stand to look at each other so they covered themselves with a leaf which represented death. They wrapped themselves in leaves which were decaying, as they were separated from the life source, the tree. In disobedience to God's request, they began to experience death. Death was not a part of God's plan for humanity.

Disobedience will always separate us from the goodness of God. Prior to what we consider the fall, Adam and Eve only knew life. All that God is and represents is life. Today we are the benefactors of life through Jesus Christ.

The thief comes only in order to steal and kill and destroy. I came that they may have and enjoy life, and have it in abundance (to the full, till it overflows).
JOHN 10:10 AMP

This chapter started with several scriptures on honor and obedience. Just as God desired Adam and Eve to honor Him, He desires us to honor and obey Him. The price of disobedience is extremely costly. In Adam's case, it cost Him everything of value; God's fellowship/intimacy, the Glory of God, provision, divine health, peace, love, and gold. I almost forgot to mention the gold in Eden, which the Bible states was good gold.

Today many Christians are living a lifestyle that is not victorious or pleasing to God because they do not obey Him. God desires us to obey and honor His word so that it will go well with us and that our lives will be filled with His goodness and provision. As we honor God, in complete submission to Him, He in return rewards us with health, peace, provision, favor, wisdom, and intimacy with Him.

The rewards for honoring God clearly outweigh the short term illusions. Disobedience tells us that everything is going to be okay because God loves me. God is obligated to honor His Word not our word. Sometimes we believe a lie and think that we no longer have to honor God's Word, but God must honor His word.

To honor God is to love God above all selfish desires. In today's society, many suffer from the "me complex syndrome". It is a syndrome that gives a person tunnel vision in which they see and care only about themselves. It is God's desire that we are to be co-laborers with Him and do the work of righteousness with Him.

When Adam, the only son of God, betrayed God, he excluded God. As Adam excluded God from his thoughts, God excluded Adam from his inheritance. Adam was the only person in the beginning who was scheduled to receive all that God owned. Yes, did you get what I just said? Adam was heir to ALL of God's possessions. Today we are heirs of God's possessions through Jesus Christ.

As we honor God, we have access to the wealth and provision of God. God withholds no good thing from those who love Him and honor Him. Honor is the key to God's heart. As we honor God, He says to Himself, "I have to honor my son or daughter". When God honors you the world takes note of it, as God does it BIG to show the world that He is God Almighty.

As we study the Word of God, we find many such as Abraham who continually honored God. Abraham only wanted God to get the credit for his joy, peace, wealth, and victory in battle. Today, God desires us to be as faithful as Abraham. Abraham was no doubt blessed, highly favored, and esteemed among kings.

God did creative and unusual miracles in Abraham's life so that all the people would know that the Living God was His God. God likes to show off His goodness in the lives of those who will honor Him. As we honor God, He guarantees that things will go well for us.

Honor is a magnet that attracts the goodness of the Blessing to chase believers down and overtake us. Honor provokes the fulfillment of the promises of God in our lives. Honor attracts the presence of God. Honor sets us before those who have the ability to confer prosperity and peace.

I am writing this from experience as I have learned to honor God in all that I do and everything that I possess. There is not anything that I own that God does not have access too. If I own it, God owns it. If God gives me an instruction I am quick to obey. I mentioned the word quick as there is no such thing as delayed obedience to God, just ask   Jonah.

Jesus is our greatest example of honoring God our Father. God was so delighted with Jesus and His obedience that God spoke from the heavens so that all who were present would know that Jesus was His son and He (God) was well pleased with Him (Jesus). Now the moment of truth has come. Is God well pleased with you? What must you do that God has instructed you to do that you have not yet done? God wants to show others that you are His and that He is well pleased with you.

ONE NEW MAN

One new man? What does this mean? The answer may be very shocking depending upon your spiritual background. As I write this I must be honest with you. I did not always know the answer that I am about to share with you.

I have attended several Bible Colleges and Universities over the years. However, even with all their great teachings and curriculums meant to educate ministers and believers not one emphasized the following truth. The understanding that everything Jesus has done and accomplished on our behalf is rooted in the revelation of One New Man.

Say what? Yes you did read it correctly. The quality and measure of the life that we experience is determined by our understanding of being one new man. JESUS DIED THAT THE JEW AND THE GENTILE WOULD BE ONE NEW MAN.

Having no hope and without God in the world. But now in Christ Jesus you who used to be far away have been brought near by the blood of Christ.
EPHESIANS 2:11-13 NET

For there is no distinction between the Jew and the Greek (Gentile), for the same Lord is Lord of all, who richly blesses all who call on him.
ROMANS 10:12 NET

Jesus through His death, burial, and resurrection created one new man. Jesus became the ultimate sacrifice that would combine the Jew and Gentile into one new being to expand the family of God.

Prior to Jesus's fulfillment of His assignment in the earth to expand the family of God, Israel was the only nation or people who had access to God. Now as one people in Jesus, God sees and receives the Jew and non-Jew the same. God no longer demonstrates partiality, as we are both one in Jesus.

Then Peter started speaking: "I now truly understand that God does not show favoritism in dealing with people, but in every nation the person who fears him and does what is right is welcomed before Him.
ACTS 10:34-35 NET

Now, as children of the Living God, we have the same access to Him and to the promises which He made to Israel's forefathers as do the Jews.

I will make my promise to you and your descendants for generations to come as an everlasting promise. I will be your God and the God of your descendants.
GENESIS 17:7 GW

God spoke to Abraham assuring Him that He will be the same God to Abraham's descendants as He was to Abraham. Now as we read the scripture in Galatians that same promise has been made unto all through Jesus.

You are all God's children by believing in Christ Jesus. Clearly, all of you who were baptized in Christ's name have clothed yourselves with Christ. There are neither Jews nor Greeks, slaves nor free people, males nor

females. You are all the same in Christ Jesus. If you belong to Christ, then you are Abraham's descendants and heirs, as God promised.
GALATIANS 3:26-29

Jesus has made it possible for all of humanity to experience the goodness of God and to be heirs of the divine will of God in this life. We do not have to die to go to Heaven to experience God's best. Jesus said on the cross "It is finished". Those three words carry the power of life and death. In the words "It is finished" is the guarantee that all mankind has been reconciled to God the Father. In those three words is the guarantee of the fulfillment of the promises.

For all of God's promises have been fulfilled in Christ with a resounding "Yes!" And through Christ, our "Amen" (which means "Yes") ascends to God for his glory.
2 CORINTHIANS 1:20 NLT

Therefore, accept each other just as Christ has accepted you so that God will be given glory. Remember that Christ came as a servant to the Jews to show that God is true to the promises he made to their ancestors. He also came so that the Gentiles might give glory to God for his mercies to them.
ROMANS 15:7-9 NLT

In Jesus the believer has access to all that Father God owns. Jesus has made us heirs of the promises God made to Abraham.

Abraham was a man found righteous in the sight of God, as he desired the true and living God. Abraham chose not to follow in the footsteps of his father and worship idols. Abraham's love for God was so sincere and genuine that God reintroduced the Blessing, which was lost by Adam to all of humanity.

God found Abraham to be a man that was faithful and loyal. There was nothing that Abraham wouldn't do for God or give to God. All that Abraham had was available to God. Prior to Abraham God had blessed them male (Adam) and female (Eve). Now through the finished work of Jesus we have received the Blessing that God originally intended for all of humanity. Prior to Jesus only Israel had access to the Blessing. The Blessing enables and empowers mankind to fulfill the purposes of God in the earth.

ONE NEW MAN PART 2

Is Israel still relevant today? The answer is YES. Does God still honor His covenant with Israel? The answer is YES. You may say I was taught that God was done with Israel. That statement is NOT true. If God were done with Israel He would be done with the Church, as the Church is an extension of Israel. Say what? You may have even been told that the Church replaced Israel. Well, that is not true either. Israel is the root of the Church.

So I ask, "Has God rejected his people Israel?" That's unthinkable! Consider this. I'm an Israelite myself, a descendant of Abraham from the tribe of Benjamin. God has not rejected his people whom he knew long ago.
ROMANS 11:1-2 GW

Anti-Semitism tries to discredit Israel and remove anything perceived Jewish from Christianity. The spirit of Anti-Semitism has crept into the teachings of the Church and the hearts of believers. Therefore, a lot of anti-Jewish teachings and replacement theology has gone forth to separate Israel and the Church.

When we study the foundation of Christianity, we find it was birthed with an all-Jewish congregation. On the day of Pentecost the upper room was filled with Jews who believed in Jesus. Christianity without Israel would just be a powerless religion.

As we see in Romans chapter 11, Israel is the root and the Church is the branch. The Apostle Paul whose assignment was to the Gentile believers explained to them that God's plan for Israel had not changed. Paul goes on to explain that the Church and Gentile believers should remain humble, as they were the branch and not the root.

Paul explained to the Church that the Gentile believers did not become the root when Jesus died on the cross. That would have meant that they had replaced Israel. Instead, he taught them that the Israel was still the root and foundation for Judeo Christianity.

Israel is the foundation or root of the Church as it has a history and a heritage with God. No other people or nation has as much experience with the Almighty God as Israel. Israel is our example of the love God has for His people. Israel is our example of the power that the Blessing exhibits which we now have through Jesus as the seed of Abraham.

As one new man in Christ Jesus we have been destined to do great exploits in our generation. As one new man we are the infusion of the former and the latter. We are a mixture of the Word and Spirit. In us resides the self -same spirit that raised Jesus Christ from the dead. Jesus was one new man as He was the Word made flesh, filled with the Holy Spirit.

And the Word was made flesh, and dwelt among us, (and we beheld his glory, the glory as of the only begotten of the Father,) full of grace and truth.
JOHN 1:14 KJ

For he is sent by God. He speaks God's words, for God gives him the Spirit without limit.
JOHN 3:34 NLT

Jesus was the first-born which God used as a ransom to release humanity from bondage. In one act of kindness on the cross Jesus restored humanity to its rightful place in the family of God.

For God knew his people in advance, and he chose them to become like his Son, so that his Son would be the first-born among many brothers and sisters.
ROMANS 8:29 NLT

Today we can call the same God of Israel our God and loving Father. Today we can experience the benefits of sonship that Israel experienced for generations. In this our God acknowledges us as His very own just as he does Israel.

The name, Israel, means to reign and rule like God. Israel was a type and shadow of the original man, who was made in the image and likeness of Almighty God. God found a small group of people to whom he could demonstrate and manifest Himself through so that other nations would know that He is the only true and Living God.

God used Israel and still does today to show the world that He alone is God. As believers come into the revelation of who they really are in Christ, they too will be used at a national level as Israel is, so that unbelievers around the world would receive Jesus as Lord.

IT'S YOURS

The promises of God are real. There are many believers who have become discouraged throughout the years because they have not seen the manifestation of many things prayed for, confessed, or written in the Bible. As a follower of Jesus Christ, we know that God is not a person that He would lie.

God is not a man, that he should lie, nor a human being, that he should change his mind. Has he said, will he not do it? Or has he spoken, and will he not make it happen?
NUMBERS 23:19 NET

At some point in our relationship with God, we must be real with ourselves and ask ourselves: "What is delaying or aborting the Word of God from being evident in my life?"

It is this question that positions one for a breakthrough. However, many people never ask themselves why their breakthrough is not happening or they unknowingly settle for some religious answer which is just as deceptive.

For example: "Pastor, I have been tithing but nothing
                is happening,"
Pastor's response: "Well you know the good Lord knows what we need and he won't give us more than we can handle."

The above scenario is all too common in the Body of Christ. Let's do this again.

"Pastor, I have been tithing, but nothing is happening,"
Pastor's response: "How are you living your life outside of

Church? Are you being honest in your giving? Are you expecting God to produce a harvest? Are you open and receptive to God giving you money- making ideas that you have to act on?"

We must take the Word of God seriously and position ourselves to be the benefactor of the promises.

> *You want what you don't have, so you scheme and kill to get it. You are jealous of what others have, but you can't get it, so you fight and wage war to take it away from them. Yet you don't have what you want because you don't ask God for it. And even when you ask, you don't get it because your motives are all wrong— you want only what will give you pleasure.*
> JAMES 4:2-3 NLT

It is time to start asking God what is the hindrance to the promises manifesting in your life. Make a decision that you will not settle for the lies of the devil and/or answers of religion. God wants to hear your voice. God wants to know that you really believe and desire his Word to come to pass in your life.

> *Put me in remembrance; let us argue together; set forth your case, that you may be proved right.*
> ISAIAH 43:26 ESV

God enjoys when His beloved brings His word before Him in the courts of Heaven. God is a God of justice and He will reward you according to your case. There are many people who will not petition God for personal desires and wants because they are afraid that He will respond in anger or not at all. One must know that God is a loving Father to us and that He cares about our well-being.

Come, let's talk this over, says the Lord; no matter how deep the stain of your sins, I can take it out and make you as clean as freshly fallen snow. Even if you are stained as red as crimson, I can make you white as wool! If you will only let me help you, if you will only obey, then I will make you rich!
ISAIAH 1:18-19 TLB

God wants the reality of his Word to become real in our life. It is time for you to talk with Father God and come to a conclusion that will position you for the manifestation of the promises of God.

"My thoughts are not your thoughts, and my ways are not your ways," declares the Lord. "Just as the heavens are higher than the earth, so my ways are higher than your ways, and my thoughts are higher than your thoughts." "Rain and snow come down from the sky." They do not go back again until they water the earth. They make it sprout and grow so that it produces seed for farmers and food for people to eat. My word, which comes from my mouth, is like the rain and snow. It will not come back to me without results. It will accomplish whatever I want and achieve whatever I send it to do."
ISAIAH 55:8-11 GW

One must come to the realization in their relationship with God that His Word is absolute. There is no benefit in doubting God. However, when you question God with the right motives and de-sires you will experience the manifestation of great gains in this life.

Prayer

Father God, I come humbly and boldly before your throne of grace. I am seeking the understanding I need to access the power to release the promises of your Word in my life. As your beloved child, I know that you are a covenant- keeping Father. I know that you desire only the best for me. I know the promises that were made to Abraham are the same promises that have been made available to me. Father, speak forth that I may hear and respond accordingly that you may be glorified in my life, in Jesus's name, Amen.

GENERATIONAL

The promise that God made to Abraham was generational. It was not just for Abraham and his family, but to all those who would choose to pursue the living God. Abraham was a man found faithful and favorable in the sight of God.

Abraham, like King David, was truly a man after the heart of God. God found Abraham's hunger for relationship well-pleasing and acceptable. Abraham was discovered to be trustworthy with the ways and revelation of God.

How blessed is the man who finds wisdom and the man who gains understanding.
PROVERBS 3:13

But the wisdom from above is first pure, then peaceable, gentle, reasonable, full of mercy and good fruits, unwavering, without hypocrisy.
JAMES 3:17

Know that wisdom is thus for your soul; If you find it, then there will be a future, and your hope will not be cut off.
PROVERBS 24:14

Wisdom along with an inheritance is good and an advantage to those who see the sun. For wisdom is protection just as money is protection, But the advantage of knowledge is that wisdom preserves the lives of its possessors.
ECCLESIASTES 7:11-12

If the axe is dull and he does not sharpen its edge, then he must exert more strength. Wisdom has the advantage of giving success.

ECCLESIASTES 10:10

"But do people know where to find wisdom? Where can they find understanding? No one knows where to find it, for it is not found among the living. 'It is not here,' says the ocean. 'Nor is it here,' says the sea. It cannot be bought with gold. It cannot be purchased with silver. It's worth more than all the gold of Ophir, greater than precious onyx or lapis lazuli. Wisdom is more valuable than gold and crystal. It cannot be purchased with jewels mounted in fine gold.

Coral and jasper are worthless in trying to get it. The price of wisdom is far above rubies. Precious peridotite from Ethiopia cannot be exchanged for it. It's worth more than the purest gold. "But do people know where to find wisdom?

Where can they find understanding? It is hidden from the eyes of all humanity. Even the sharp-eyed birds in the sky cannot discover it. Destruction and Death say, 'We've heard only rumors of where wisdom can be found.'

"God alone understands the way to wisdom; he knows where it can be found, for He looks throughout the whole earth and sees everything under the heavens.

He decided how hard the winds should blow and how much rain should fall. He made the laws for the rain and laid out a path for the lightning.

Then He saw wisdom and evaluated it. He set it in place and examined it thoroughly. And this is what he says to all humanity:

'The fear of the Lord is true wisdom; to forsake evil is real understanding.'" JOB 28:12-28 NLT

Wisdom is the key to maximizing the power of the Blessing. For ages many have tried to imitate or to counterfeit the Blessing. The Blessing will always cause a person to prosper and succeed in unexplainable ways. The Blessing is not limited to science or what we consider the physical realm. The Blessing has always been supernatural and continues to accomplish its purpose with style.

The wisdom of God demands obedience. This is the key to a successful life. Often times, we find ourselves in disobedience to the instructions of God as we don't fully understand His plan. The rewards of God have nothing to do with our understanding of His instructions, but everything to do with our obedience to His Word.

A severe famine now struck the land, as had happened before in Abraham's time. So Isaac moved to Gerar, where Abimelech, king of the Philistines, lived.
The LORD appeared to Isaac and said, "Do not go down to Egypt, but do as I tell you. Live here as a foreigner in this land, and I will be with you and bless you. I hereby confirm that I will give all these lands to you and your descendants, just as I solemnly promised Abraham, your father.
I will cause your descendants to become as numerous as the stars of the sky, and I will give them all these lands. And through your descendants all the nations of the earth will be blessed.
I will do this because Abraham listened to me and obeyed

all my requirements, commands, decrees, and instructions." So Isaac stayed in Gerar.

When the men who lived there asked Isaac about his wife, Rebekah, he said, "She is my sister." He was afraid to say, "She is my wife." He thought, "They will kill me to get her, because she is so beautiful." But some time later, Abimelech, king of the Philistines, looked out his window and saw Isaac caressing Rebekah.

Immediately, Abimelech called for Isaac and exclaimed, "She is obviously your wife! Why did you say, 'She is my sister'?"

"Because I was afraid someone would kill me to get her from me," Isaac replied.

"How could you do this to us?" Abimelech exclaimed. "One of my people might easily have taken your wife and slept with her, and you would have made us guilty of great sin."

Then Abimelech issued a public proclamation: "Anyone who touches this man or his wife will be put to death!"

When Isaac planted his crops that year, he harvested a hundred times more grain than he planted, for the LORD blessed him. GENESIS 26: 1-12

ISRAEL

One may ask, "What does Israel have to do with the manifestation of the promises of God? This may be a shock to you, but everything for without Israel there would be no access to the promises.

It's through our knowledge of Israel and the covenant that God made with Israel that one can place a demand on the manifestation of the promises. There are many people who have been taught that the blessings of God are automatic.

If the above statement was true, there would not have been a need for this written guide, nor would you have had a need to read this guide, because all the promises of God would have already come to pass in your life.

When the Church began separating itself from Israel, the Church was repositioned for a relationship with God without power and provision. The nation of Israel and the Jewish people have the greatest revelation of God's power to provide, defend, protect, and honor His Word.

As a result of the Church at large separating itself from Israel, the Church was separated from necessary experience, understanding, relationship, and revelation. No other people in history, like the Israelites, have been able to rebuild repeatedly after being evicted from one country after another.

It is the revelation that was passed down, to the people of Israel, from generation to generation that has caused the Jewish people to be resilient, innovative, creative, and wealthy. As a result of Jesus going to the cross on Calvary, we are no longer multiple people groups, but are one.

There are neither Jews nor Greeks, slaves nor free people, males nor females. You are all the same in Christ Jesus.
GALATIANS 3:28 GW

Jesus came and created unity between the Jews and non-Jews so that there would be no distinction between the two concerning relationship, power, presence, provision, miracles, health, ideas, or wealth.

For there is no distinction between Jew and Greek: for the same [Lord] is Lord of all, and is rich unto all that call upon him.
ROMANS 10:12 ASV

It is the will of God that the revelation that the Jews have received and that has been activated throughout the centuries be shared and taught in the present-day Churches. In order for the Body of Christ to experience the fullness of the promises and the Blessing, we must embrace the Jewish people and the Nation of Israel. Israel from a biblical perspective has been the foundation for believers to build faith and to desire a relationship with Father God.

It is important to remember that you were not Jewish physically, however, those who called themselves "the circumcised," because of what they had done to their bodies--have called you "the uncircumcised." Also, at that time you were without Christ. You were excluded from citizenship in Israel, and the pledges God made in his

promise were foreign to you. You had no hope and were
in the world without God.

EPHESIANS 2:11-12 GW

Therefore, remember that at one time you were Gentiles
(heathens) in the flesh, called Uncircumcision by those
who called themselves Circumcision, in the flesh made
by human hands. [Remember] that you were at that time
separated (living apart) from Christ [excluded from all part
in Him], utterly estranged and outlawed from the rights of
Israel as a nation, and strangers with no share in the sa-
cred compacts of the [Messianic] promise [with no knowl-
edge of or right in God's agreements, His covenants].
And you had no hope (no promise); you were in
the world without God.

EPHESIANS 2:11-12 AMP

This is a good place to pause and start praising God for Jesus and for the salvation that we have through Him. We must acknowledge and accept the Jewish people as our sisters and brothers in Christ Jesus. We have to change our mindset from thinking that only the Jews are privileged to the production and consumption of wealth by owning businesses, producing movies, creating inventions, and various other innovations.

We are the children of the same God as the Jewish people, and we too are privileged to obtain the promises of God through Jesus Christ. We must change our thinking to embrace the power of God, so that His power is manifested and becomes evident in our lives, as it has for centuries for the Nation of Israel and the Jewish people.

*But now that this faith has come, we are no longer under
the control of a guardian. You are all God's children by
believing in Christ Jesus. Clearly, all of you who were baptized in Christ's name have clothed yourselves with Christ.
There are neither Jews nor Greeks, slaves nor free people,
males nor females. You are all the same in Christ Jesus.
If you belong to Christ, then you are Abraham's
descendants and heirs, as God promised.*

GALATIANS 3:25-29 GW

If you are not shouting right now, you need a fresh touch of the
Holy Spirit. Jesus has set us free from bondage, sin, shame,
guilt, poverty, sickness, and being outsiders. We are now children of the Most High God and heirs to the promises God made
to Abraham. Thank God for being a generational God who desires to bless everyone in the family.

*But when the right time came, God sent his Son, born of a
woman, subject to the law. God sent him to buy freedom
for us who were slaves to the law, so that he could adopt
us as his very own children. And because we are his children, God has sent the Spirit of his Son into our hearts,
prompting us to call out, "Abba, Father." Now you are no
longer a slave but God's own child. And since you are
his child, God has made you his heir.*

GALATIANS 4:4-7 NLT

Do you acknowledge yourself as a child of God? Do you see
yourself as an heir of God? As a child and heir of God, one is
entitled to access God and all that he owns. God is the largest
shareholder in both the spirit and natural realms.

If one lacks understanding of what God owns, that individual cannot rightfully place a demand on it to be manifest in their life. It is through personal revelation of one's position in Christ, and knowledge of the covenant that God made with Abraham that a person's request is made with total assurance for an expectant outcome.

Prayer

Father God, I ask that you grant me a spirit of wisdom and revelation of insight into the knowledge of Christ. Open the eyes of my heart and flood it with your light that I will know and understand the hope which you have called me. I desire that you fill me with so much understanding that I will know the unlimited greatness of your power in and for all who believe. I continually make room and allow the power of God to be demonstrated in my life, in Jesus's name, Amen.

PERCEPTION

In order for the fullness of the promises of God to be manifest in your life, one must overcome guilt. It does not benefit one to be guilty or ashamed for desiring a demonstration of the goodness of God in one's life. Guilt or shame will hinder God's power.

It is important to know that God will demonstrate His power where there is rejoicing and giving of thanks. God wants to be known in the lives of His children as a great and mighty God.

The children of Israel referred to God as The Lord My Provider. God is attracted to individuals and atmospheres where He is celebrated and not just tolerated.

>**Give thanks to the LORD, for he is good;**
>**his love endures forever.**
>PSALM 107:1 NIV

In unison when the trumpeters and the singers were to make themselves heard with one voice to praise and to glorify the LORD, and when they lifted up their voice accompanied by trumpets and cymbals and instruments of music, and when they praised the LORD saying," He indeed is good for His loving kindness is everlasting," then the house, the house of the LORD, was filled with a cloud, so that the priests could not stand to minister because of the cloud, for the glory of the LORD filled the house of God.
2 CHRONICLES 5:13-14 NASB

A lifestyle of praise keeps the windows of blessing open to manifest the promises of God. Religion, referring to the traditions of men, has robbed people of the promises and power of God. God is more eager to demonstrate His power than we are willing to ask.

Whatever you ask in My name, that will I do, so that the Father may be glorified in the Son. If you ask Me anything in My name, I will do it.
JOHN 14:13-14 NASB

There are many individuals who fear asking God for anything as they were always told to be content and not be greedy. To ask God to fulfill His word in our lives is our reasonable service as children of God. The Gospel of "make it stretch" and "you don't need all that," has created a wedge between God's people and the promises that He desires for us to possess. The promises are sitting across the street saying "I want to come to you, but you will not allow me because of your doubt and unbelief." The promises of God are voice- activated and must be spoken in faith.

Jesus said to them, "Have faith in God! I can guarantee this truth: This is what will be done for someone who doesn't doubt, but believes what he says will happen: He can say to this mountain, "Be uprooted and thrown into the sea," and it will be done for him. That's why I tell you to have faith that you have already received whatever you pray for, and it will be yours.
MARK 11:22-24 GW

But when you ask, you must believe and not doubt, because the one who doubts is like a wave of the sea, blown and tossed by the wind. That person should not expect to receive anything from the Lord.
JAMES 1:6-7 NIV

One must be fully convinced that the Word of God is true and that God desires to manifest the Word of God in our lives. Any doubt will abort the Word of God from being a living reality in our lives.

Jesus said to him, "If you can believe, all things are possible to him who believes." Immediately the father of the child cried out and said with tears, "Lord, I believe; help my unbelief!" When Jesus saw that the people came running together, He rebuked the unclean spirit, saying to it: "Deaf and dumb spirit, I command you, come out of him and enter him no more!"
MARK 9:23-25 NKJV

As you continue reading there will be promises you can speak into existence daily. The Word of God mixed with faith produces manifestation.

How Rich is Your Soul?

Beloved, I pray that you may prosper in all things and be in health, just as your soul prospers.

3 JOHN 1:2 NKJ

How rich is your soul? Your soul prosperity directly influences your ability to prosper in the other areas of life. Yes, when the soul is lacking, other areas of our life and being will lack as well. The will of Father God is that we feed our soul His word; His word must become a living reality in our lives.

God created the human race as tri-part beings. We are Spirit (God in us), Soul (mind, will, & emotions), and Body (where we live). 3 John 1:2 is a powerful scripture that is so overlooked and undervalued in our lives. As a result, many are not prospering in life because their soul is not prospering.

Let's examine the will of God here for a moment. The Soul consists of three parts mind, will, and emotions. To prosper in my soul is to prosper in my mind, will, and emotions. The mind is the control tower where thoughts are created, examined, and executed. As our mind prospers, we position our thoughts to prosper.

It is through our mind that we give the entrance of desires access into our life. The things which we rehearse in the mind and meditate on will be that which we will allow to become present in our lives. What are you feeding your mind? Is it the Word of God or the lies and deceptions that are seen on the television or heard on the radio? God instructed Joshua to meditate on His Word.

This Book of the Law shall not depart from your mouth,
but you shall meditate in it day and night, that you may
observe to do according to all that is written in it.
For then you will make your way prosperous,
and then you will have good success.
JOSHUA 1:8 NKJV

God wanted Joshua to condition his soul with His Word. As we condition our Soul with the Word of God, we will make room for it to be a living reality in our life. This verse says that after you have meditated in the Word day and night and are obedient to the voice of the Lord, you will make your way prosperous and have good success. The Word of God conditions the believer for prosperity inwardly and outwardly. In addition, it conditions one to experience good success in his/her life.

The mind is being renewed as one meditates on the Word. As the mind is being renewed, it is accepting as truth that which it is being renewed with. People act on that which we perceive to be true or a truth. Not only does our mind prosper, but so does our will. As we continue to meditate on the Word of God, it influences our likes, tastes, and desires. Meditating on the Word causes our will to be in sync with the will of God.

In addition to our soul and will being influenced by the Word of God, so are our emotions. Our emotions are the cheerleaders or motivators that encourage us in our determined desire. If the desire which we want is based in the Word of God, our will is in sync with His Will, and our emotions will assure us that we made the right decision.

Emotions send forth frequencies throughout the body, giving

that desire permission to come into existence. Our emotions are powerful and can create force fields or barriers that can prohibit certain things from having access into our life.

Also, simultaneously our emotions can create a magnetic force to attract and accelerate the manifestation of a desire. As mentioned early in this chapter, "How rich is your soul?" What changes can you make in your life to increase the prosperity of your soul? As your soul prospers, the other areas of your life will prosper also.

THIS MIND

Let this mind be in you, which was also in Christ Jesus.
PHILIPPIANS 2:5 KJV

Whose mind are you living through? What mind is determining how you will fare in life? What mind is determining what you will become in life? What mind is determining how you take action in life?

The will of Father God is that we operate in the same mind that operated in Christ. Say what! How can that be possible? Jesus was the son of God. Well guess what, you are NOW a child of God with the same access and rights that were available to Jesus.

Jesus is our example of why we must continually renew our minds with the Word of God. Even though Jesus was flesh like us, he succeeded in fulfilling His assignment because He did not allow external factors or the opinions of others to determine His decisions. The decisions we make should be rooted in the Word of God.

When Satan came and made Jesus several offers to worship and work for him, Jesus refused by saying, "It is written." Jesus referenced the Word of God in that situation. When you are in situations do you reference the Word of God?

Then Jesus said to them, "When you lift up the Son of Man, then you will know that I am He, and that I do nothing of Myself; but as My Father taught Me, I speak these things. And He who sent Me is with Me. The Father has

not left Me alone, for I always do those
things that please Him."
JOHN 8:28 -29 NKJ

Then Jesus answered and said to them, "Most assuredly,
I say to you, the Son can do nothing of Himself, but what
He sees the Father do; for whatever He does, the Son
also does in like manner."
JOHN 5:19 NKJ

Jesus is our greatest example of living from above while here on earth. Yes, we are in the earth, but we are citizens from another Kingdom. Therefore, we should not subject ourselves to thinking according to worldly traditions that minimize the power of God.

And so, dear brothers and sisters, I plead with you to give
your bodies to God because of all he has done for you.
Let them be a living and holy sacrifice—the kind he will
find acceptable. This is truly the way to worship him. Don't
copy the behavior and customs of this world, but let God
transform you into a new person by changing the way you
think. Then you will learn to know God's will for you,
which is good and pleasing and perfect.'
ROMANS 12:1-2 NLT

To think as one from this world is to not acknowledge the power, will, and presence of God. God is insulted when we look at a situation from the world-mind, which is limited in its capacity to think, perceive, and imagine. Let's examine the story of Jesus feeding the multitude.

When Jesus landed and saw a large crowd, he had compassion on them and healed their sick.

As evening approached, the disciples came to him and said, "This is a remote place, and it's already getting late. Send the crowds away, so they can go to the villages and buy themselves some food." Jesus replied, "They do not need to go away. You give them something to eat."

"We have here only five loaves of bread and two fish," they answered.

"Bring them here to me," he said. And he directed the people to sit down on the grass. Taking the five loaves and the two fish and looking up to heaven, he gave thanks and broke the loaves.

Then he gave them to the disciples, and the disciples gave them to the people. They all ate and were satisfied, and the disciples picked up twelve basketfuls of broken pieces that were left over. The number of those who ate was about five thousand men, besides women and children.

MATHEW 14:14-21 NIV

In this story the world-minds of the disciples said it is late, we are in a remote area, and we need to send these people away so they can get something to eat on their own. Jesus responded, "They don't need to go away. You give them something to eat." This blew the disciples' minds as they could only see and embrace the limitation of 5 loaves and 2 fish. Jesus perceived that there was no shortage and there was enough for everyone.

The world-mind was saying, "What are you talking about? Look at all these people. Man, can't you see there has to be over 20,000 people here and you want to tease them with this little boy's lunch?" Jesus responded, "Give me the loaves and fish". The disciples looked at Him through their world-minds and said, "I can't believe this brother is about to eat that little boy's lunch." They were partially correct. Jesus took the food and planted it in the soil of Heaven for an immediate unlimited harvest. The scripture says Jesus held the loaves and fish and blessed them.

Jesus planted the bread and fish as a seed with an expected harvest. When He blessed it, He transferred it into the realm of the eternal where time does not exist. The Blessing of God that we have on our lives supersedes time and gives us access to the now of God.

The now of God for every believer's life is to experience Heaven on earth. There are many people who have been taught the following: to do without; to settle; to be content with what they have; or to not expect more. After these traditions, people begin to lose confidence in the Word of God and misquote the Word of God, in order to justify their doubt in the power of the Blessing and the promises of God.

Jesus taught us in Matthew 6 that instead of accepting what the World has to offer that we should call Heaven down. Jesus taught us to accept the reality of Heaven on earth as our way of life.

Pray along these lines: 'Our Father in heaven, we honor your holy name. We ask that your kingdom will come now. May your will be done here on earth, just as it is in heaven.'

MATTHEW 6:9-10 TLB

You should begin to speak Heaven into your life and situations. Don't limit God through   shortage and poverty thinking. As you call Heaven down, you make room for the infinite power of God to demonstrate and change your current reality. God is NOT limited in His potential or power.

Determine within yourself to call down Heaven in every area of your life. Just say it like this, "God, I need a manifestation of Heaven in my life. I need your kingdom to come and reign in my life. God, I will no longer settle for limitations in life through the world- mind. I have the mind of Christ."

Declare that Heaven come down, and then declare where you need a manifestation, i.e., bank account, business, work place, marriage, relationships, health, or home. Don't be shy. You are the son or daughter of the Most High God!

Let us then approach God's throne of grace with confidence, so that we may receive mercy and find grace to help us in our time of need.
HEBREWS 4:16 NIV

THE BLESSING

So God created man in His own image; in the image of
God He created him; male and female He created them.
Then God blessed them, and God said to them, "Be fruit-
ful and multiply; fill the earth and subdue it; have dominion
over the fish of the sea, over the birds of the air, and
over every living thing that moves on the earth."
GENESIS 1:27-28 NKJV

God created male and female after His image and likeness. After God created the human race, the scripture says, "Then God
blessed them." The blessing that God bestowed upon the first
family was not like what many have perceived as the blessing
today.

Many believe that the Blessing is the receiving of something ma-
terial or a tangible experience. I suggest that those are a result of
the Blessing. After God pronounced the Blessing, cars, clothes,
money, and houses did not fall out the sky.

The first man did not get a promotion on his job or a pay increase. Don't get me wrong. There is nothing wrong with those
things. However, we should not limit or restrict the Blessing to
those types of things. In many instances, the power of the Blessing has been minimized to no avail. We serve a great God, with
immeasurable power to create and demonstrate His promises in
our lives.

Now glory be to God, who by his mighty power at work
within us is able to do far more than we would ever dare
to ask or even dream of—infinitely beyond our highest

prayers, desires, thoughts, or hopes.
EPHESIANS 3:20 TLB

Now to Him Who, by the [action of His] power that is at work within us, is able to [carry out His purpose and] do superabundantly, far over and above all that we [dare] ask or think [infinitely beyond our highest prayers, desires, thoughts, hopes, or dreams]
EPHESIANS 3:20 AMP

All I can say is don't limit God in your life. Don't limit the potential and opportunities that you can have and experience in this life. You have more going for you than you realize. We have the power of the Blessing of God at work in us, through us, and around us. The Blessing is extremely powerful and productive. The Blessing is a supernatural empowerment bestowed upon mankind by God to govern, legislate, and produce.

All that one needs to experience the best life has to offer is found within the Blessing. The Blessing has the inherent power of God to execute judgment on darkness. Darkness is all that which opposes the will of God.

In darkness is found the root of curses, sickness, disease, and poverty. The power of the Blessing is so great that it will separate a person from the power of darkness. One can struggle with curses and poverty most of one's life, but once the Blessing is pronounced and   received that person's life will reflect the goodness of God as if it had always been that way.

Then the Man said, "Let me go, for it is dawn."
But Jacob panted, "I will not let you go until you

bless me."

"What is your name?" the Man asked.

"Jacob," was the reply.

"It isn't anymore!" the Man told him. "It is Israel—one who has power with God. Because you have been strong with God, you shall prevail with men." "What is your name?" Jacob asked him.

"No, you mustn't ask," the Man told him. And he blessed him there.

GENESIS 32:26–29 TLB

If you have studied the life of Jacob prior to the Blessing given by God to him, you know then that he lived an unfulfilled life full of deceit and manipulation. The Blessing changed his life and repositioned Jacob to become the Father of Israel.

"For we are going to Bethel," he told them, "and I will build an altar there to the God who answered my prayers in the day of my distress, and was with me on my journey."

GENESIS 35:3 TLB

Upon Jacob's arrival at Bethel, en route from Paddan-aram, God appeared to him once again and blessed him.

And God said to him, "You shall no longer be called Jacob ('Grabber'), but Israel ('One who prevails with God').

I am God Almighty," the Lord said to him, "and I will cause you to be fertile and to multiply and to become a great nation, yes, many nations; many kings shall be among your descendants.

And I will pass on to you the land I gave to Abraham and Isaac.

Yes, I will give it to you and to your descendants.
GENESIS 35: 9 – 12 TLB

The Blessing gave his life meaning and purpose. Without properly understanding the Blessing one can wander through life. The Blessing is God's thoughts being released upon a person to redirect their future. The Blessing creates a future that is joyous, fulfilling, dynamic, and full of wonder. The foundation for success in life is found in the power of the Blessing.

The Bible makes some very profound statements concerning the power of the Blessing. According to scripture the Blessing can change one's financial position. Many struggle in life barely getting by because the power of the Blessing is missing.

The Blessing in the courts of Heaven executes justice for a person in want, lack, and need. The Blessing rules that poverty is guilty of tormenting a child of the Creator. Therefore all the effects of poverty must leave at once and never return. The Blessing positions a person to hear ideas from God that if acted upon will create new rivers of wealth in that person's life.

The blessing of the LORD, it maketh rich, and he
addeth no sorrow with it.
PROVERBS 10:22 KJV

Praise God! We can become rich and enjoy the benefits of the process. Many people look down on wealth. To despise wealth is to despise the Blessing. The primary function of the Blessing is to produce wealth in a person's life to influence the laws of the land by standing for righteousness and justice according to the will of God.

So even though wisdom is better than strength, those who are wise will be despised if they are poor. What they say will not be appreciated for long.
ECCLESIASTES 9:16 NLT

Today in our society we see the reality of this scripture. Hollywood and well-financed interest groups are setting the standard and the example in our culture (society). As a result, the Church at large is mocked and is not completely representing the Kingdom of God due to the misunderstanding and lack of wealth. The Body of Christ should be the example of wealth and riches. It is the Church's responsibility to set the standard in society not Hollywood.

Abraham was God's servant who was well- respected amongst nations. He was a man who loved God with his whole heart and with his possessions. There was nothing that God couldn't ask of Abraham. As a result, Abraham experienced the power of the Blessing to produce unlimited and never- ending rivers of wealth.

Abram had become very wealthy in livestock and in silver and gold.
GENESIS 13:2 NIV

The LORD has blessed my master, and he has become wealthy. The LORD has given him sheep and cattle, silver and gold, male and female slaves, camels and donkeys.
GENESIS 24:35 GW

Abraham's wealth was a result of the Blessing of God. The Lord had said to Abram, "Go from your country, your

people and your father's household to the land I will
show you. "I will make you into a great nation, and I will
bless you; I will make your name great, and you will be a
blessing. I will bless those who bless you, and whoever
curses you I will curse; and all peoples on earth will
be blessed through you."
GENESIS 12:1-3

As we continue to examine scripture, we see that God fulfilled His Word and promise to Abraham. The Bible assures us that no Word of God is without power or the ability to produce. The reason the Word of God has not produced in many people's lives is because it has not been received with a proper attitude.

I've had conversations with individuals who are strong believers of Christ that don't even accept the possibility of God making them wealthy or healing their body. They just want to make enough to meet expenses and to live comfortably.

That is an insult to the Word of God. It is one of the worst forms of selfishness masked as humility. Our nation is in the position it is because the Church lacks financial resources and influence. As a result laws are being passed to legalize sin to support the kingdom of darkness. The will of God is that the righteous be in authority.

When the godly are in authority, the people rejoice. But
when the wicked are in power, they groan.
PROVERBS 29:2 NLT

In order to create a future that is productive and beneficial for generations to come, the Church at large must become receptive to the will of God concerning wealth. Poverty will be the catalyst that eliminates the Church as we know it today.

Abraham was very wealthy and respected by kings of other countries. His wealth was used to sustain proper influence, empower the people, and finance the will of God. The Blessing of God is bigger than a paycheck in which you struggle to live from week to week. The Blessing is about a lifestyle and creating a legacy that will reign for generations to come.

Prayer

Father God, I renounce all wrong thinking concerning the Blessing and wealth. I ask for wisdom and understanding that comes from above that I may live in the power of the Blessing. I know the Blessing will make me rich without sorrows. I have the mind of Christ. Therefore, I have a right understanding of wealth and its purpose. I receive all the benefits and privileges of the Blessing now, in Jesus's name, Amen.

THE WEALTH FACTOR

Wealth, riches, and money are the most misunderstood triplets in the Body of Christ. The gospel of poverty and false humility has blinded many individuals from the will of God. I even see people make excuses to be poor by blaming some preacher or evangelist who had a moral failure. I choose not to live through someone else's experience or opinion. As for me, I will serve the Lord and make room for the Blessing in my house.

For many years I have heard that money is the root of evil. It always amazed me that the people who misquoted the scripture worked the hardest to get some money. Being scriptural, those individuals worked the curse, but confessed Jesus as Lord. What kind of theology is that? **1 Timothy 6:10 says "The love of money is root to all evils".**

This scripture is not just limited to rich people. It is inclusive, as you have just as many poor people who love money and try to mask it.

Money in itself is not good or bad. Money is a neutral medium of exchange that communicates and demonstrates. Money does not take sides, belong to one group versus another, or has any say in any person's life. We must be good stewards of money and be responsible and wise in all our dealings.

The Parable of the Bags of Gold

"Again, it will be like a man going on a journey, who called his servants and entrusted his wealth to them. To one he gave five bags of gold, to another two bags, and to another

one bag, each according to his ability. Then he went on his journey. The man who had received five bags of gold went at once and put his money to work and gained five bags more. So also, the one with two bags of gold gained two more. But the man who had received one bag went off, dug a hole in the ground and hid his master's money.

After a long time the master of those servants returned and settled accounts with them. The man who had received five bags of gold brought the other five. 'Master,' he said, 'you entrusted me with five bags of gold. See, I have gained five more.'

"His master replied, 'Well done, good and faithful servant! You have been faithful with a few things; I will put you in charge of many things. Come and share your master's happiness!'

"The man with two bags of gold also came. 'Master,' he said, 'you entrusted me with two bags of gold; see, I have gained two more.'

"His master replied, 'Well done, good and faithful servant! You have been faithful with a few things; I will put you in charge of many things. Come and share your master's happiness!'

"Then the man who had received one bag of gold came. 'Master,' he said, 'I knew that you are a hard man, harvesting where you have not sown and gathering where you have not scattered seed. So I was afraid and went out and hid your gold in the ground. See, here is what belongs to you.'

"His master replied, 'You wicked, lazy servant! So you knew that I harvest where I have not sown and gather where I have not scattered seed? Well then, you should have put my money on deposit with the bankers, so that when I re-

turned I would have received it back with interest.
"So take the bag of gold from him and give it to the one who
has ten bags. For whoever has will be given more, and they
will have an abundance. Whoever does not have, even what
they have will be taken from them. And throw that worth-
less servant outside, into the darkness, where there will be
weeping and gnashing of teeth." MATTHEW 25:14-30 NIV

In this parable we see that a businessman entrusted varying sums of money with three individuals. The businessman had an expectation that these three individuals would be wise and increase the money they were given.

Yes, two of the investors did just that, and found very rewarding opportunities for their money to grow. In verse 16 there is some beautiful language stated like this "The one who received five bags went at once and put his money to work." We were not created by Father God to work for money or things.

There is more to life than the labor for money. When one walks with God and is open to the desires of God, God will give them money- generating ideas that will create lasting wealth and not a paycheck.

We were not created to be lazy servants. As we study the parable, the investor who buried the gold in the ground was considered wicked and lazy. Why? He was given an opportunity to change his circumstances just like many today. However, he did nothing. Instead he hid himself from the responsibility of a new reality.

Many people give and ask God for increase and financial

breakthrough. However, when the opportunity is there, they refuse to take action. The Word of God tells us that faith without works is dead. Many people die in a temporary situation by taking a permanent stand to do nothing. What idea has God given you to change your life and the lives of others? What have you done with it?

Do you have a fear of what others will think? Get over it. People with low self- confidence and esteem are going to talk about you regardless of what you do or don't do. God desires for his children to prosper as it brings glory unto Him.

> *Let them shout for joy, and be glad, that favor my righteous cause: yea, let them say continually, Let the LORD be magnified, which hath pleasure in the prosperity of his servant.*
> PSALM 35:27 KJV

Do you rejoice as you prosper? God finds pleasure in seeing you prosper. Do you see prospering as a good and beneficial event in life? Or do you see it as a means to pay your bills only? Prospering should be fun and satisfying. The gateway to wealth is to accept money as good. Also, wealth and riches should be viewed as a reward for demonstrating your talents in the marketplace. As we position our thinking in sync with the mind of Christ, we will walk in the wealth of God on earth.

THE GOSPEL

Traditionally what has been taught in many denominations and churches has not been the Gospel of Jesus Christ. Instead, it has been man's ideals of how to connect with and please God through false humility and works of the flesh. The message of the gospel that   has been typically taught has not benefited the congregations as much as it has the corporate offices and the pockets of the top ten. This has been an issue even before the days of Jesus's ministry.

You Pharisees and teachers of the Law of Moses are in for trouble! You're nothing but show-offs. You lock people out of the Kingdom of Heaven. You won't go in yourselves, and you keep others from going in. You are in trouble! You are supposed to lead others, but you are blind. You teach that it doesn't matter if a person swears by the temple. But you say that it does matter if someone swears by the gold in the temple.
MATTHEW 23:13-15 CEV

The doctrines that have been taught in our churches and society have not always been that of God. The Gospel which Apostle Paul taught had great power and had reproducible results that transformed nations.

And my speech and my preaching was not with enticing words of man's wisdom, but in demonstration of the Spirit and of power: That your faith should not stand in the wisdom of men, but the power of God.
1 CORINTHIANS 2:4-5 KJV

The gospel, which we see primarily, taught today is man's intellect and charisma. We have a generation of believers that have itching ears. They want a gospel that is conducive to their destructive lifestyle.

For the time will come when people will not put up with sound doctrine. Instead, to suit their own desires, they will gather around them a great number of teachers to say what their itching ears want to hear.
2 TIMOTHY 4:3 NIV

The devil is more willing to accommodate than one realizes. The devil capitalizes on an individual's lack of hunger and thirst for more of God. As a result, the gospel of bondage and oppression has been able to spread across nations, hindering the creative power of God. This counterfeit message has placed people under the control of the Kingdom of darkness. The assignment of the Kingdom of darkness is to occupy and oppress the people of God.

You know that God anointed Jesus from Nazareth with the Holy Spirit and power. Jesus went everywhere and did good things, such as healing everyone who was under the devil's power. Jesus did these things because God was with him.
ACTS 10:38 GW

The message that Jesus taught was demonstrated with the power of God. As Jesus taught, there were healings, deliverances, and supernatural demonstrations of provision. The Gospel of the Kingdom of God is not rooted in intellect.

For the Kingdom of God is not a matter of talk
but in power.
1 CORINTHIANS 4:20 KJV

As my spiritual Father would say, "Anyone can preach in America, as there is no expectation of power." When we go to the Temple of God, one should be strengthened in power to exercise it in everyday life.

There should be a demonstration of power during the worship service. Today, however, there is a great absence of power in the Church. The lack of power is a direct reflection of the lack of relationship with Israel.

I have heard many ministers say that Israel has been replaced by the Church and has no relevant significance today. That is a lie of the devil to strip the Church of power and purpose. The Church is an extension of Israel. It was never supposed to become organized religion. Jesus's greatest opposition was from the leaders of organized religion.

In order for the power of God to be active in the Church today, the leaders must repent for being anti-Israel and embrace the Jewish people. It is impossible to fulfill scripture if you don't embrace the people we are supposed to win to Christ.

Did God's people stumble and fall beyond recovery?
Of course not! They were disobedient, so God made
salvation available to the Gentiles (non- Jews). But he
wanted his own people (Jews) to become jealous
and claim it for themselves.'
ROMANS 11:11 NLT

To love Israel is to love God. Israel is an extension of God. You can't have God without Israel or Israel without God. It's like saying I would like a glass of water without the wet. In like manner, Israel is a portal or gateway which God could use to reveal Himself in the earth. As a result, salvation was made available to the non-Jew so that we could fellowship and partake of the goodness of God.

For you are a people holy to the LORD your God.
The LORD your God has chosen you to be a people for
his treasured possession, out of all the peoples who
are on the face of the earth.
DEUTERONOMY 7:6 ESV

They are the people of Israel, chosen to be God's adopted
children. God revealed his glory to them. He made cov-
enants with them and gave them his law. He gave them
the privilege of worshiping him and receiving his
wonderful promises.
ROMANS 9:4 NLT

Please examine your heart toward Israel. To love Israel is more than just giving monetary donations and tangible goods. Loving Israel is having a right heart toward the nation of   Israel and the Jewish people.

Pray for peace in Jerusalem. May all who
love this city prosper.
PSALM 122:6 NLT

GENESIS

The Lord said to Abram, "Leave your land, your relatives, and your father's home. Go to the land that I will show you. I will make you a great nation, I will bless you. I will make your name great, and you will be a blessing. I will bless those who bless you, and whoever curses you, I will curse. Through you every family on earth will be blessed."
GENESIS 12:1-3 GW

The Blessing is God's way of materializing Himself in the earth. The Blessing is the evidence of the reality of His existence. Through the blessing God reveals His ability to demonstrate His goodness in one's life. The goodness of God is revealed in the promise of the Blessing. In the power of the Blessing one has been given a legal right to enforce the will of God in his or her life. God has already made the ruling which states that the promises are yes and amen to each believer.

O taste and see that the LORD is good: blessed is the man that trusteth in him.
PSALM 34:8 KJV

Choose to live in the Blessing and know the reality of the goodness of God daily. The Blessing was the gateway to the restoration of all which Adam lost in the Garden. God promised Abraham that He would bless him. The Blessing God pronounced upon Abraham was a supernatural empowerment to prosper, succeed, and legislate (to exercise dominion & authority).

And God blessed them, and God said unto them, Be fruitful, and multiply, and replenish the earth, and subdue it: and have dominion over the fish of the sea, and over the fowl of the air, and over every living thing that moveth upon the earth.

GENESIS 1:28 KJV

The first family is the model for what the power of the Blessing will enable one to accomplish in life. The Blessing gave them super power abilities to stay on top and reign in life.

The Blessing empowered humanity to:
1. Be fruitful – reproduce
2. Multiply – increase
3. Replenish – create
4. Subdue – conquer and overcome
5. Have Dominion – rule like God

Abraham had the ability to enforce the desire and will of God in the earth through the Blessing. Everything that Abraham touched, prospered and succeeded. Abraham gained favor among Kings and nations for they knew that God was with Abraham. The Blessing is evidence that God is with us. Abraham, the Father of Faith, is our greatest example of allowing all that the Blessing is to become evident in one's life.

Abraham gained the advantage in battle and won as a result of the Blessing. He was able to rescue his nephew Lot and recover all. The Blessing caused his body and Sarah's body to be restored in order that they would birth a son named Isaac.

The same Blessing that was upon Abraham was upon Isaac as well. The Blessing caused Isaac to prosper and succeed during the great depression and famine of his time. While others were experiencing extremely challenging and difficult circumstances, Isaac was not because God blessed him. That same Blessing that was upon Abraham and Isaac is now upon you and me through Jesus Christ.

And there was a famine in the land, beside the first famine that was in the days of Abraham. And Isaac went unto Abimelech king of the Philistines unto Gerar.

And the Lord appeared unto him, and said, Go not down into Egypt; dwell in the land which I shall tell thee of:

Sojourn in this land, and I will be with thee, and will bless thee; for unto thee, and unto thy seed, I will give all these countries, and I will perform the oath which I sware unto Abraham thy father;

Then Isaac sowed in that land, and received in the same year a hundredfold: and the Lord blessed him.

And the man waxed great, and went forward, and grew until he became very great:

For he had possession of flocks, and possession of herds, and great store of servants: and the Philistines envied him.

GENESIS 26:1-3, 12 – 14 KJV

WHAT WAS LOST?

The first man was the Spirit of God housed in a body formed from the dust of the ground. The original body, which housed the presence of God, only knew the atmosphere of Heaven. In Heaven all things reflect the reality of who God is and His will. The original body was conditioned to live in an environment which reflected the atmosphere of Heaven. The will of God from the beginning has been for the human race to experience Heaven on earth.

The Lord God planted a garden in Eden, in the east.
That's where he put the man whom he had formed.
GENESIS 2:8 GW

Eden was an extension of Heaven in the earth. It was created for the human race to inhabit and enjoy. The word, Eden, has not been fully communicated in our culture that we would embrace the fullness of the desires of God. The Hebraic meaning of Eden is delight, finery, luxury, and pleasure. Eden was an opulent and extravagant dwelling place for the presence of God. Eden was the place God frequented to visit the first family.

Eden has been commonly communicated as the garden
which God told Adam to tend and keep. In the garden
God commissioned Adam to discover his possibilities
and potential as the new life form on the earth. It was in
the garden God gave Adam the assignment of expanding
Eden to cover the whole earth. And they heard the voice of
the LORD God walking in the garden in the cool of the day:
and Adam and his wife hid themselves from the presence

of the LORD God amongst the trees of the garden.
GENESIS 3:8 KJV

Prior to Adam's disobedience to the instructions of God in the garden located in Eden, man's capacity to believe, receive, and legislate was without boundaries. The ability of mankind to create was just as that of God through the Blessing. The Blessing was the sign of God in the earth.

Through the power of the Blessing mankind had the ability to duplicate Heaven on the earth. The voice of mankind in the beginning had the DNA of God. The essence of God was in Adam's voice, which enabled him to speak as if it were God speaking. The creative power of God was released through the voice of Adam. In the beginning all Adam had for a reference point was God.

In the beginning was the Word, and the Word was with God, and the Word was God. He was with God in the beginning. Through him all things were made; without him nothing was made that has been made.
JOHN 1:1-3

All that Adam was able to accomplish he did through his relationship with God. God was the first teacher to the man He created in His likeness and image. In the beginning all God had to work with was His word. God taught Adam how to use his words to exercise dominion, to create, and to enforce the Blessing. To enforce the Blessing is to speak as God desires it to be.

Today we see laws and legislation enacted in every form of government. A law is a set of words, which will create a reality once mutually agreed upon and it is signed into law. Once those defined set of words or drafted legislation is law, it then must be enforced by the proper authorities for it to work.

The born- again believer is the proper authority to legislate the Word of God in the earth. As a person decrees, pronounces, and blesses, so shall it be.

You will also decree a thing, and it will be established for you; And light will shine on your ways.
JOB 22:28 NASB

As it is written, "I have made you the father of many nations." Abraham acted in faith when he stood in the presence of God, who gives life to the dead and calls into existence things that don't yet exist.
ROMANS 4:17 ISV

If speaking the Word worked for God, it will work for us. From the beginning God created it so that the human race would succeed. We must choose to believe God and trust Him without fear or doubt of the outcome.

It is the same with my word. I send it out, and it always produces fruit. It will accomplish all I want it to, and it will prosper everywhere I send it.
ISAIAH 55:11 NLT

When you enforce the power of the Blessing, your life, surroundings, and affairs are governed by the Word of God. Jesus is our greatest example of one who only speaks as Father God spoke it.

For I did not speak on My own initiative, but the Father Himself who sent Me has given Me a commandment as to what to say and what to speak. "I know that His commandment is eternal life; therefore the things I speak, I speak just as the Father has told Me."
JOHN 12:49 – 50 NASB

Jesus said to the Jews, "I can guarantee this truth: The Son cannot do anything on his own. He can do only what he sees the Father doing. Indeed, the Son does exactly what the Father does.
JOHN 5:19 GW

Jesus's desire was to have the reality God desired by only saying what the Father said. As believers we must learn to discipline our thoughts and speech to create the reality of God in our lives.

ORIGINAL INTENT

The plan of God was for man to rule and reign in the earth. It was never God's idea that man be exposed to the kingdom of darkness and the curses. The only reality God desired for humanity was Heaven on earth. Adam and Eve lost their identity, dominion, and authority in disobedience to the will of God. As a result humanity lost its ability to think, see, imagine, create, and legislate like God.

All that which composed the Blessing was no longer available to humanity. Now man must work a foreign system to meet the needs of his family. The system or ways of doing things in Eden were no longer available to the human race. Prior to the Fall mankind did not work as we know work today. In the beginning man fulfilled his purpose and assignment.

Then the LORD God took the man and put him into the Garden of Eden to cultivate it and keep it.
GENESIS 2:15 NASB

The power of the Blessing made that which man needed conveniently accessible to fulfill his purpose. Today we have to ask ourselves if we are fulfilling our purpose or working to meet our perceived needs. The purpose of the Blessing was to enable each individual with the ability to fulfill his or her assignment on earth.

Today we live in a society where many are not fulfilling their assignments because they have bowed to foreign kingdoms of darkness to meet their needs. God has the ability and resources to meet our needs beyond our wildest dreams. In Matthew 6,

Jesus asked the people, "What is your problem? You call your-selves children of God, but you do everything just as those who have no faith or relationship with God."

Later in the chapter Jesus tells us to seek the Kingdom of God and His right way of doing things. Jesus assured us that as we seek the Kingdom of God that the things we so desire would become available to us.

And why worry about your clothes? Look at the field lilies! They don't worry about theirs. Yet King Solomon in all his glory was not clothed as beautifully as they. And if God cares so wonderfully for flowers that are here today and gone tomorrow, won't he more surely care for you, O men of little faith?
So don't worry at all about having enough food and cloth-ing. Why be like the heathen? For they take pride in all these things and are deeply concerned about them. But your heavenly Father already knows perfectly well that you need them, and he will give them to you if you give him first place in your life and live as he wants you to.
So don't be anxious about tomorrow. God will take care of your tomorrow too. Live one day at a time.
MATTHEW 6:28 – 34 TLB

Jesus has brought us back into divine alignment with the original plans of God. Now mankind has the ability to function, as did the first man. Jesus was the second Adam who came to demonstrate to the world what the first Adam had the ability to do. The Bible tells us that Jesus healed all those who were oppressed or tor-mented of the devil. Jesus executed justice on behalf of each of those individuals. He enforced the will of God by healing the sick.

We as the third Adam must accept our position and possibilities through the restoring work of Jesus Christ.

ACCESS GRANTED

All that which was lost concerning the Blessing has been restored to every born- again believer through the finished work of Jesus Christ. No longer do we have to fellowship with poverty, lack, need, or despair. We now have all that God promised in the Blessing to Abraham to us through salvation.

Prior to the coming of Christ, God found a man named Abram who was faithful. God made a covenant with him to bless him and all his descendants. This covenant or agreement was binding for all generations that would occupy the earth.

I will establish my covenant as an everlasting covenant between me and you and your descendants after you for the generations to come, to be your God and the God of your descendants after you.
GENESIS 17:7 NIV

The descendants of Abram who later became Abraham lost sight of the purpose of the Blessing. God blessed Abraham and his seed to provoke the idol worshipers to jealousy. This jealousy was to provoke the idol worshipers to seek and worship the God of Abraham. The God of Abraham was the living God who was faithful to all those who called Him Lord.

The Blessing is a supernatural empowerment of God for the human race to succeed in life. The Blessing gives one the power and ability to overcome obstacles, limitations, hindrances, doubt, fear, curses, and strongholds which work to oppose the good that God desires to be known in one's life.

The Blessing gives one the capacity to produce and think as the first man did prior to the Fall. The mindset of Adam was created from the reality of the presence of God in Eden. Adam only knew the unexplainable and inexhaustible power of God. The Blessing will override that which is perceived as fact to create the reality of God.

God endorses the Blessing so much, that as we release words of blessing from our mouths it is as if God Almighty is saying them Himself. Everything in the universe takes note of what is being said when it is in accordance with the mindset of God. The angels who are constantly at work in the invisible realm work with passion and urgency to make that which is invisible to become visible.

Examine the desires of your heart and the words which you release into the atmosphere. Are those words charging the atmosphere for a demonstration of the power or God? Our words create an atmosphere that produces rain in our lives. What type of rain is pouring down on you? Are you experiencing showers of blessings or curses (continuous setbacks, failures, disappointments, demonic attacks and troubles)?

THE RESTORED MIND

In the Fall of mankind the mindset of God was lost. In the beginning the only way God's greatest creation could think was the way God thought. The level of consciousness and awareness the first man walked in is beyond comprehension. The original man utilized his mind to capacity. The mind that Adam operated in had no comprehension of lack, want, need, shortage, sickness, disease, death, decay, famine, violence, or chaos. He operated in the highest understanding of God.

Now we must learn to operate at a greater level of understanding through the renewing of our minds after one accepts Jesus as Lord. Now we have to recondition our level of thinking with the Word of God. This is why it is important for a believer to worship the Father God. It is in worship where the reality of all that God is, is revealed. In worship, God removes the limits that have been applied to the imagination and mind.

In the Church today you hear very little about imagination, as its purpose has been hijacked and perverted. The imagination is the eye of the spirit through which one sees and frames the future. The imagination is the gateway to creating a new reality. It is in the   imagination that we see things the way God sees them. It is in the imagination that creativity and solutions are birthed.

To pervert the imagination and discount its purpose is to hinder the creative power of God. Imagination had its origin in the beginning in the mind of God. The purpose of our imagination is to rehearse the thoughts of God. We are to imagine the Word of God as the reality of God in our lives. As we do we give access or make room for it to become the reality in our lives.

Faith convinces us that God created the world through his Word. This means what can be seen was made by something that could not be seen.
HEBREWS 11:3 GW

God is the imagination. God is the infinite source of creativity. All that was created in the beginning was a reflection of the inner thoughts or imagination of God. As He saw it within Himself as thought, He began to speak it into being. Thought is a powerful instrument to give something entrance into one's life. The Bible commands one to cast down every vain imagination and guard one's thoughts.

My son, pay attention to my words. Bend your ear to my speech. Don't let them slip from your sight. Guard them in your mind. They are life to those who find them, and healing for their entire body. More than anything you guard, protect your mind, for life flows from it.
PROVERBS 4:20-23 (COMMON ENGLISH BIBLE)

Casting down imaginations, and every high thing that exalteth itself against the knowledge of God, and bringing into captivity every thought to the obedience of Christ.
2 CORINTHIANS 10:5 KJV

Our imagination is the highest form of thought. The imagination is the Spirit of God revealing the future and desires of the heart. The future is to be meditated upon and spoken into existence.

It is vitally important that one guards the use of the imagination for right and good purposes. Each individual has the power and capability to become one with their imagination. Jesus only used his spiritual eyes to see the actions of the Father and duplicate them in the earth.

So Jesus explained, "I tell you the truth, the Son can do nothing by himself. He does only what he sees the Father doing. Whatever the Father does, the Son also does.
JOHN 5:19 NLT

The power of the imagination is beyond understanding. As you were growing up, there may have been people who couldn't embrace your imaginative ability and would tell you to stop thinking like that or to curb your wild imagination. The first and foremost purpose of the imagination is to bring you into right understanding of the potential you have in God.

It is by the power of the imagination that mankind has sent individuals and satellites into outer space. Daily the imagination is creating and giving birth to new ideas and concepts. The mobile phone began as an idea in the mind of Martin Cooper. Today mobile phones have become the primary means of voice communication in many countries.

Many have been robbed of God experiences by not utilizing their imagination to embrace and empower God possibilities in their life. The possibilities of the creative power of God are limitless. As we are growing in the awareness of the reality of God that Adam knew prior to the Fall, we must employ our imagination to expand our capacity for more of God.

I use my imagination often to keep the promises and desires of God before me. I have taken so many self-imposed limitations off my life by reinforcing God desires in my imagination. I continually make room for the power of God to be demonstrated in my life by seeing it the way God sees it through my imagination.

When I feel like I am getting sick, I start seeing and feeling myself as if I were healed. The symptoms leave and the healing is manifested. Last week while on a plane to Chicago, the pilot instructed us to prepare for severe turbulence. I had to make up my mind as to which image I was going to embrace. I chose to embrace an image of a smooth flight without turbulence. As I imagined so it was. My flight to Chicago was peaceful.

I have taken the limits off my life imposed by others. I refuse to allow small thinkers to bring me down to their level of consciousness. I continually grow in the revelation of what God is capable of doing by employing the power of my imagination.

The very things that we imagine are coming into being. I give access to that which will bring glory to the Father permission to exist in my life through my imagination. The imagination is the initiator of change and the beginning of creation. Allow yourself to enjoy the power and presence of your imagination in divine oneness with Father God.

A good man out of the good treasure of his heart bringeth forth that which is good; and an evil man out of the evil treasure of his heart bringeth forth that which is evil: for of the abundance of the heart his mouth speaketh.
LUKE 6:45 KJV

THE MARK OF GOD

It is God's desire that the mark of God be upon his people. The evidence that the God of Abraham, Isaac, and Jacob is your God is the Blessing.

The LORD spoke to Moses, saying, "Speak to Aaron and his sons, saying, Thus you shall bless the people of Israel: you shall say to them,
The LORD bless you and keep you; the LORD make his face to shine upon you and be gracious to you; the LORD lift up his countenance upon you and give you peace. So shall they put my name upon the people of Israel, and I will bless them. NUMBERS 6:23 – 27 ESV

It was God's desire in the days of Moses that the Children of Israel be recognized as the Children of the true and living God. As with Abraham, God wanted Abraham and those associated with him to stand out as those in divine relationship with the true and living God.

Abraham through the Blessing was the proof that God was real. God materially manifested himself in the life of Abraham to the point he became extremely wealthy. Abraham's ability to amass wealth was rooted in his obedience and relationship with God. Abraham only wanted God to have the credit for prospering him. He was a faithful and loyal friend that only desired God to receive the credit for prospering him.

And so it happened just as the Scriptures say: "Abraham believed God, and God counted him as righteous because

of his faith." He was even called the friend of God.
JAMES 2:23 NLT

The heart of Abraham was consistently mindful of the love and promises of God. Abraham's family and those who were a part of his household experienced the goodness of God through Abraham's hunger for God's way of living. As we focus on living in the reality of the will of God, we too will experience the goodness of God. Those who are connected to us will experience God's goodness also.

The goodness of God is to provoke the unbeliever to believe in the God of Abraham, Isaac, and Jacob. The goodness of God is a demonstration of His love for His people. God wants His people to enter in to peace and rest. As a result of the goodness of God in the lives of believers, others should desire to accept Jesus as Lord.

MA'ASER

"Bring the entire tithe into the storehouse so that there may be food in my temple. Test me in this matter," says the LORD who rules over all, "to see if I will not open for you the windows of heaven and pour out for you a blessing until there is no room for it all."
MALACHI 3:10 NET

I am honored that Father God would allow me to share what I am about to share with you in this chapter. I pray that as you read, you are open to the voice of God to guide you and mentor you in the understanding that has been absent from the body of Christ.

Our society has accepted a culture and system that is not aligned with the Kingdom of Heaven. As a result we have adapted to a counterfeit way of life. The way of life which we have become accustomed to is designed to distract and keep our minds from thinking that there could possibly be more to life.

As I mentioned several times in this writing Jesus came that we may have life more abundantly. As we look around there is nothing abundant or enjoyable in life today, as people are stressing out and worried about how they will make it mentally, emotionally, physically, and financially.

In the Kingdom of Heaven we cast our cares on Him (God) for He cares for us. As we participate in the principle and promise of tithing we are casting our cares on Him. In Malachi, God makes us a promise within a promise to protect us and prosper us so that others will see that He kept His promise to those who tithe.

In my experience and opinion the tithe is the miracle cure to the pressures presented to us in everyday life. The tithe to the Temple is one promise that I have acted on and experienced a demonstration of its reality in my life for many years. I am thankful that I gained understanding in my early twenties. This understanding and practice has guided me from success to success. The tithe to the Temple is one of our greatest partners in success.

The Temple tithe creates an atmosphere for an impartation of creative ideas and concepts. People are always trying to come up with the next big idea or best- selling gadget. As one who has an approved patent by the United States Patent and Trademark Office, great ideas are golden. Even good ideas will rake in hundreds of thousands of dollars.

I know people go to great lengths to obtain ideas and talents that will create for them wealth. I have watched documentaries where people confess they sold their soul to the devil for fame and fortune. I was reading online an article by entrepreneur.com that some inventors had near death experiences to get ideas. Here is a quote from that same article mentioning Steve Jobs the founder of Apple and Yoshiro Nakamatsu creator of the floppy disk.

"Steve Jobs, for example, routinely sat on toilets, dangling his bare feet in the water while he came up with new ideas, and Yoshiro Nakamatsu (inventor of the floppy disc) would dive deep under water until his brain was deprived of oxygen, then write his ideas on an underwater sticky pad." (http://www.entrepreneur. com/article/249931?et_cid=256352&et_rid=23752926)

It is really mind- blowing what people will do capture a thought that will benefit society and create wealth. I will continue to work the principle of the tithe as it doesn't require a near death experience. Tithing only requires humility and obedience. One of my favorite quotes says "If you are willing and obedient you will eat the good things of the land" or "Experience the best life has to offer".

No other people group in history has kept, honored, and participated in the appointed times of God as have the Jewish people. The Jewish people have made honoring God during the feast of the Lord a part of their reasonable service. Giving in the way God desires has been proven to work on their behalf.

People envy the wealth and success of the Jewish people. Their success and wealth comes from the age-old principles taught by Abraham and Moses. Even Jesus endorsed those principles in scripture and enforced them for New Testament believers by accepting the crown of thorns.

On the cross Jesus exchanged His wealth for what would have been our lack and poverty. To embrace lack and poverty as a mindset is to deny the death, burial, and resurrection of Jesus. Jesus is either Lord and King over every area of our life or we lie. As the scriptures say," They worship Me with their mouths, but their hearts are far from Me."

Jesus has paved the way and become the door that all of humanity could have the God of Israel as their God. No longer is there a separating barrier. We can now ALL experience the promises and goodness of God as heirs and children of God.

The promises of the tithe work for both the Jew and non-Jew as God is no respecter of persons.

I recently watched a really good movie on the abundance factor and one of the individual's interviewed made a very bold, but profound statement. He said, "Abundance is all around us, except in church".

His statement may be controversial. Yet it is a fact that for decades the Church at large has not been prosperous. The truth is Jesus came that we would live an abundant life with access to all the good God has made available to us in the earth.

For the purpose of this writing I can't go into great depth on why the poverty doctrine has gained acceptance and traction in the Church. It was not God endorsed or God's will. It was created by a group of leaders to control and manipulate the people.

History shows these leaders created a platform for people to look to them and not to God. In a sense these leaders desired to be a god to the people, in order to carry out their own agenda. They had to strip people of their pride, self- worth, confidence, creativity, and wealth.

So what I call the plantation doctrine was birthed to keep people in their place and dependent on a system built by deception, corruption, chaos, and greed. You may ask why I use such strong language to describe mainstream religion. The purpose of mainstream religion was never to connect people to God.

Jesus came that we might have life and have it more abundantly through a progressive and intimate relationship with the Father.

Father God always desired to have a family to fellowship with and love. God desires nothing more than a real relationship with you and me.

You may ask, "What does my relationship with God have to do with the tithe? In the next several paragraphs you will learn what many have known for ages that have caused them to prosper and succeed despite world conditions.

The word tithe as we commonly refer to it is derived from the Hebrew word Ma'aser. This is a very old word, not commonly used a lot today but it still fulfills the purpose God assigned to it. Ma' aser, in short, is defined as the prescription to wealth or the guarantee that one will become wealthy. I know that many have been taken advantage with their giving and tithing over the years. However, that does not justify us not trusting God or obeying His Word to tithe.

The tithe is very powerful, honorable, and significant to God. God receives the tithe as a form of worship, act of obedience, a demonstration of faith, and an act of love. As we study scripture, Abraham tithed out of love and desire to please God. I want you to understand that the manner in which the tithe is given is just as important as giving the tithe in itself.

Each of you should give whatever you have decided. You shouldn't be sorry that you gave or feel forced to give, since God loves a cheerful giver.
2 CORINTHIANS 9:7 GW

The condition of the heart is everything to God when we tithe or give offering. The tithe awakens the favor and goodness of God in one's life. As a tither for over 15 years I can attest that it works if you work it. I enjoy tithing and look forward to the many opportunities to give: at Church, in special meetings, to charities, the poor, or to a worthy cause in someone's life.

Giving cheerfully says to God, I trust you no matter what. You are my source and supply. Being faithful in your giving says to God, I know you are faithful, therefore I can be faithful. God responds to our faithfulness with His promise and grace.

God responds by opening the heavens and releasing His wisdom and thoughts so that it would become our wisdom and thoughts. In the thoughts of God are divine instructions and creative ideas to create and attract wealth.

Most people think a lack of money in their life is the problem. However, that is not correct. A lack of money may be a fact of the matter, but the truth of the matter is a lack of wisdom. The wisdom of God will always attract the wealth and prosperity of God. King Solomon pleased God with his request for wisdom and instruction to lead the Children of Israel.

That night God appeared to Solomon and said, "What do you want? Ask, and I will give it to you!"
Solomon replied to God, "You showed great and faithful love to David, my father, and now you have made me king in his place. O LORD God, please continue to keep your promise to David my father, for you have made me king over a people as numerous as the dust of the earth! Give me the wisdom and knowledge to lead them properly, for who could possibly govern this great people of yours?"
God said to Solomon, "Because your greatest desire is to

help your people, and you did not ask for wealth, riches, fame, or even the death of your enemies or a long life, but rather you asked for wisdom and knowledge to properly govern my people— I will certainly give you the wisdom and knowledge you requested. But I will also give you wealth, riches, and fame such as no other king has had before you or will ever have in the future!" 2 CHRONICLES 1:7-12

So often when we make the mistake of going straight for the money, we miss wisdom. To succeed in life God's way we have to have wisdom from God. In Malachi 3:10, God promises to give us wisdom as we bring the tithe into the Temple. In scripture God says, "There will be food in my house." The word food there is revealed knowledge.

God declares that as we are faithful in tithing in the Temple He will fill the atmosphere with creative ideas and opportunities that if acted upon will produce, generate, and create wealth. The thoughts of God in themselves are always prosperous. As we accept and embrace the thoughts of God, those thoughts prosper us.

God delights in the prosperity of those who go forward with His ideas in mind. As we act on the ideas of God, it creates an opportunity for God to prove himself and demonstrate His love in our lives. As a result of our obedience we create an opportunity to give God praise for His wonderful works. The praise that we can give God is what causes God to delight in the prosperity of those who serve Him.

Your willingness to participate in the will of God is the key to living in the promises of the tithe. I have from my own experiences found the promises of the tithe to be true. I now have creative ideas and concepts that are currently being developed to enter the market place.

I could have found a thousand excuses why it will not work, but I chose to believe one truth, "God can't fail". I have experienced favor upon favor as I have gone forward in obedience. The resources and right people have come into my life, as I have needed them to accomplish various tasks and activities.

New doors and opportunities that I could never have imagined have been opened to me because of the promise of the tithe. I believe if I were not practicing this principal I would not be where I am now in life. I testify that the goodness of God is waiting to overtake anyone who will dare to believe and act.

Now that you have the prescription to wealth and prosperity that works beyond and despite world conditions, what will you do with it?

Congratulations

I celebrate your courage to challenge the status quo and continue to break free of limiting thoughts concerning who you are and the Blessing. It is your time to begin walking in the manifested promises of the Blessing. It is your time to experience favor and grace working with you to secure your health, happiness, and prosperity.

You should begin seeing yourself with wealth and doing things that will forever change the lives of people. Also, you should visualize yourself enjoying the benefits of wealth. It's okay to have your dream home, dream car, dream business, dream charity, dream vacation, and so on. God wants you to enjoy life and to have the best life has to offer.

Money is a good assistant in helping one to enjoy life. Choose to imagine the possibilities that will be available to you as a result of the Blessing at work in your life. Each day for the next thirty days renew your mind to the word of God concerning the power of the Blessing and favor.

Read and meditate upon the daily scripture word by word, if necessary. Decree out loud the affirmation and confirmation several times during the day and night. Allow God to reveal Himself to you through His word.

> **'Wealth and riches shall be in his house: and his righteousness endureth forever.'**
> PSALM 112:3 KJV

Foundation Scripture: **Genesis 1:27-28 NKJ**

So God created mankind in His own image; in the image of God He created him; male and female He created them. Then God blessed them, and God said to them, "Be fruitful and multiply; fill the earth and subdue it; have dominion over the fish of the sea, over the birds of the air, and over every living thing that moves on the earth."

Day 1 – Genesis 5:2 ISV

Creating them male and female, he blessed them and called them humans when he created them.

Affirmation

I am God's greatest creation on the earth. The creative power of God is in me. My life is a constant demonstration of the power of the Blessing.

Confirmation

I am blessed.

Day 2 – Leviticus 26:9 NIV

I will look on you with favor and make you fruitful and increase your numbers, and I will keep my covenant with you.

Affirmation

I have the favor of God at work in my life. I have been empowered to succeed in life. God keeps His promises with me.

Confirmation

I am favor.

Day 3 – Proverbs 16:15 NIV

When a king's face brightens, it means life; his favor is like a rain cloud in spring.

Affirmation

I have favor with the King of Kings. I have access to the good of the land. I live my best life now.

Confirmation

I am access.

Day 4 – Luke 1:28 GW

When the angel entered her home, he greeted her and said, "You are favored by the Lord! The Lord is with you.

Affirmation

God is on my side. Favor has been applied. I am well pleasing and acceptable to God.

Confirmation

I am God's favored child.

Day 5 – Deuteronomy 28:1 NLT

If you fully obey the Lord your God and carefully keep all his commands that I am giving you today, the Lord your God will set you high above all the nations of the world.

Affirmation

I am obedient to the Word of God. I am an active participant in the will of God for my life. My faith has works that correspond with the promises of God.

Confirmation

I am humble in all my ways.

Day 6 – Deuteronomy 28:8 NLT

The Lord will guarantee a blessing on everything you do and will fill your storehouses with grain. The Lord your God will bless you in the land he is giving you.

Affirmation

I have the blessing of God at work in my life. Everything that I set my hands to prospers and succeeds. I am extremely blessed to help others to succeed in life.

Confirmation

I am the blessing.

Day 7 – Deuteronomy 6:4 GW

Listen, Israel: The Lord is our God. The Lord is the only God.

Affirmation

I surrender all that I am to all that God is. God is my loving father, guide, and mentor.

Confirmation

I am God's child.

Day 8 – Deuteronomy 6:5 GW

Love the Lord your God with all your heart, with all your soul, and with all your strength.

Affirmation

I love the Lord my God. I love the Lord with all my heart, soul, and strength.

Confirmation

I am love.

Day 9 – Psalm 41:11 NLT (Emphasis)

I know you are pleased with me, for you have not let my enemies or negative experiences triumph over me.

Affirmation

God is pleased with me. I am more than a conqueror. God is with me leading and guiding from success to success.

Confirmation

I am victory.

Day 10 – Genesis 24:35 ISV

The LORD has greatly blessed my master, so that he has become wealthy. He has provided him sheep and cattle, silver and gold, male and female servants, camels and donkeys.

Affirmation

I am greatly blessed by God Almighty. I am continually increasing more and more. I have unlimited streams of income and revenue pouring into my life.

Confirmation

I am wealth.

Day 11 – Proverbs 10:22 NLT

The blessing of the LORD makes a person rich, and he adds no sorrow with it.

Affirmation

The blessing of the Lord makes me rich and adds no sorrow. The blessing of God empowers me to be fruitful and multiply. I rejoice always in the Blessing of God.

Confirmation

I am rich.

Day 12 – Matthew 6:9 TLB

Pray along these lines: Our Father in heaven, we honor your holy name.

Affirmation

God is my Father. I honor Him always. God is actively involved in my life.

Confirmation

I am a child of Father God.

Day 13 – Matthew 6:10 ONM

Your Kingdom must now come: your will must be done right now, as in Heaven also on Earth.

Affirmation

My life is a constant demonstration of the reality of Heaven. Heaven is my reality on earth. The will of God is active in my life.

Confirmation

I am Heaven on earth.

Day 14 – Matthew 6:11 ONM

You (God) must now give us today the things necessary for our existence.

Affirmation

Today I have fresh revelation and understanding to succeed in the affairs of life. I have all things that pertain to life and godliness. I lack no good thing.

Confirmation

I am the wisdom of God

Day 15 – Matthew 6:24 TLB

You cannot serve two masters: God and money. For you will hate one and love the other, or else the other way around.

Affirmation

I am in right standing with God. I serve the Lord God and him only. Money is my servant and serves me well.

Confirmation

I am one with God.

Day 16 – Matthew 6:25 TLB

So my counsel is: Don't worry about things—food, drink, and clothes. For you already have life and a body—and they are far more important than what to eat and wear.

Affirmation

My life overflows with the peace of God. I have all my needs met. I do not worry, as God is my source for all good things.

Confirmation

I am continuously at peace.

Day 17 – Matthew 6:30

Now if God so clothes the grass of the field, which today is, and tomorrow is thrown into the oven, will He not much more clothe you, O you of little faith?

Affirmation

My God always comes through. All my needs are met. I am strong in faith.

Confirmation

I am faith.

Day 18 – Matthew 6:33 NKJV

But seek first the kingdom of God and His righteousness, and all these things shall be added to you.

Affirmation

I continually seek and pursue the Kingdom of God. I am the

righteousness of God in the earth. God adds all good things unto me.

Confirmation
I am a citizen of the Kingdom of God.

Day 19 – Matthew 6:34 TLB
So don't be anxious about tomorrow. God will take care of your tomorrow too. Live one day at a time.

Affirmation
I am always at peace. God is my guide and source in life. All that I need has been made available to me.

Confirmation
I am abundantly supplied always.

Day 20 – Deuteronomy 8:18 ESV
You shall remember the LORD your God, for it is he who gives you power to get wealth, that he may confirm his covenant that he swore to your fathers, as it is this day.

Affirmation
I am in covenant with God Almighty. The indwelling presence of God causes me to increase more and more. I remember the Lord always.

Confirmation
I am wealth.

Day 21 – Genesis 26:12 NIV
Isaac planted crops in that land and the same year reaped a hundredfold, because the LORD blessed him.

Affirmation
The hundred-fold blessing is upon me. Everything I put my hands to prospers and succeeds.

Confirmation
I have been consumed by the Blessing.

Day 22 – Malachi 3:10 NET
Bring the entire tithe into the storehouse so that there may be food in my temple. "Test me in this matter," says the LORD who rules over all, "to see if I will not open for you the windows of heaven and pour out for you a blessing until there is no room for it all."

Affirmation
I continually bring my tithes to the House of God. As a tither the windows of Heaven are open over my life. God always gives me money-making ideas that bless me and others.

Confirmation
I am a tither.

Day 23 – Leviticus 27:30 NIV
A tithe of everything from the land, whether grain from the soil or fruit from the trees, belongs to the LORD; it is holy to the LORD.

Affirmation
I am a steward of the wealth of God. I am faithful in all that God entrusts me with. I bring to the Lord that which is holy.

Confirmation
I am worship.

Day 24 – Proverbs 3:9 NKJV

Honor the Lord with your wealth and with the first and best part of all your income. Then your barns will be full, and your vats will overflow with fresh wine.

Affirmation

I continually honor the Lord with my wealth. I bring to God that which He desires. All that I have increases more and more.

Confirmation

I am a worshipper.

Day 25 – Philippians 4:18 NKJV

Indeed I have all and abound. I am full, having received from Epaphroditus the things sent from you, a sweet-smelling aroma, an acceptable sacrifice, well pleasing to God.

Affirmation

I have the heart of a giver. I continually give to the Lord which is sweet, acceptable, and pleasing. I worship the Lord always in spirit and truth.

Confirmation

I am faithfulness.

Day 26 – Philippians 4:19 NLT

And this same God who takes care of me will supply all your needs from His glorious riches, which have been given to us in Christ Jesus.

Affirmation

My God supplies all my needs. I live in constant abundance as God always fulfills his Word in my life. My life is a constant demonstration of the Word of God.

Confirmation

I am God's beloved

Day 27 – Psalm 23:1 NIV

The LORD is my shepherd. I am never in need.

Affirmation

God's word is true in my life. I am never in need. God is my guide in the affairs of life. I lack nothing in this life.

Confirmation

I am prosperity.

Day 28 – 2 Corinthians 9:8 NLT

And God will generously provide all you need. Then you will always have everything you need and plenty left over to share with others.

Affirmation

My God will generously supply all that I need and more. I always have more than enough to share. The goodness of God is evident in my life.

Confirmation

I am more than enough through Christ Jesus.

Day 29 – Psalm 34:9-10 AMP

O fear the Lord, you His saints [revere and worship Him]! For there is no want to those who truly revere and worship Him with godly fear. The young lions lack food and suffer hunger, but they who seek (inquire of and require) the Lord [by right of their need and on the authority of His Word], none of them shall lack any beneficial thing.

Affirmation

I worship the Lord in spirit and truth. I acknowledge and inquire of God in all that I do. God continually leads me in the path of righteousness and plenty.

Confirmation

I am honor.

Day 30 – James 2:26 NKJV

For as the body without the spirit is dead, so faith without works is dead also.

Affirmation

I have a right image or picture for my desires. I demonstrate the corresponding works that will make my invisible desires visible.

Confirmation

I am faith in action.

Day 31 – Ephesians 2:10 NLT

For we are God's masterpiece. He has created us anew in Christ Jesus, so we can do the good things He planned for us long ago.

Affirmation

I am uniquely and wonderfully made in the image of God Almighty. I embrace and enjoy my individuality. I love who I am and who I am becoming in Christ Jesus.

Confirmation

I am the best version of me.

APPENDIX

1. Eden http://www.abarimpublications.com/Meaning/Eden.html#.
U6mi2ty4mll

Abarim Publications Theological Dictionary

NOTES

NOTES

NOTES